CALIFORNIA'S

Sierra Nevada

BY

AMERICAN & WORLD GEOGRAPHIC PUBLISHING

This book is dedicated to John Wight of
Orinda, California, who first showed me the
Sierra more than twenty years ago.

Library of Congress Cataloging-in-Publication Data

Wuerthner, George.
    California's Sierra Nevada / George Wuerthner.
      p. cm.
    ISBN 1-56037-036-X
    1. Sierra Nevada (Calif. and Nev.)--Geography.
    2. Sierra Nevada (Calif. and Nev.)--History.
    I. Title.
F868.S5W84   1993
979.4'4--dc20   93-3567

Text and photography © 1993 George Wuerthner
© 1993 American & World Geographic Publishing
P.O. Box 5630, Helena, MT 59604

Printed in Korea

CONTENTS

This page: Near Mono Pass, Yosemite National Park.
Facing page: Zumwalt Meadows in Kings Canyon National Park, South Fork of the Kings River.
Title page: Duck Lake in the John Muir Wilderness, Inyo National Forest.

Front cover: North along the crest of the Sierra Nevada from the summit of Mt. Whitney, Sequoia National Park.
Back cover, top: Half Dome from Glacier Point, Yosemite National Park.
Bottom: The General Lee Sequoia in Kings Canyon National Park.

Jeffrey pine at Glen Alpine Creek in the Desolation Wilderness, Tahoe Basin National Forest.

INTRODUCTION

"If we looked to the east we saw on the other side of the plain at a distance of some thirty leagues a great Sierra Nevada, white from the summit to the skirts, and running diagonally almost from south-southeast to north-northwest."

Thus did Pedro Font, a Spanish Franciscan missionary, describe the range of mountains he saw in April 1776 from a hill near San Francisco Bay. At the time Font was merely giving a descriptive name to a mountain range seen from a distance. Little did he appreciate that the snowy mountains he saw made up one of the major ranges in North America.

The Sierra Nevada, a massive block of granite that rises steeply along its eastern escarpment, is wider and higher than any other mountain range in the lower 48 states. In total, the range encompasses 15.5 million acres—an area equal to the states of Vermont, New Hampshire and Connecticut combined. Imposed over the range are several political and management boundaries, including 18 counties, portions of nine national forests, and three national parks. Private holdings comprise 30 percent of these mountains. The remaining 70 percent is under public ownership—52 percent is administered by the U.S. Forest Service, ten percent is national parks, seven percent is managed by the Bureau of Land Management (BLM), and state, county and local governments control the final one percent.

This is a mountain range of superlatives. It is one of the longest continuous mountain ranges in the United States, with one of the most extensive alpine uplands in America. The Sierra Nevada has Lake Tahoe at 1,685 feet deep, the tenth-deepest lake in the world and third deepest in North America. Kings Canyon, which reaches a depth of 8,240 feet at one point, is, according to some, the deepest canyon in the United States, surpassing the Grand Canyon's

Above: Poppies by Coulterville in Mother Lode country.
Right: Looking south from Trailcrest on the John Muir Trail, Sequoia National Park.

View from Mt. Hoffman to Clouds Rest and Half Dome in Yosemite National Park.

greatest depth by several thousand feet. Yosemite Falls cascades 2,425 feet—the third-highest falls in the world. Three other falls in Yosemite National Park rank in the top ten globally. Mt. Whitney, at 14,495 feet, is the highest point in the lower 48 states. The soaring eastern escarpment of the range leaps more than two miles above the Owens Valley, rising from Lone Pine at 3,733 feet to Whitney's 14,495-foot summit on the Sierran crest. This represents the maximum relief of any mountain mass in the lower 48 states.

The Sierra is not only a towering mountain barrier, but also a broad one. Averaging between 50 and 80 miles in width, it is a significant obstacle to everything from weather masses to road builders. Although the main crest of the range lies near its eastern margin, there are numerous ridges and sub-crests that branch off

the main divide, many with their own names—Silver Divide, Cathedral Range, Glacier Divide, Ritter Range, Great Western Divide and so on. It is this jumble of peaks seen from any high summit that gives the Sierra its special beauty and sense of immensity.

California's Sierra Nevada is not only wide, but is of the longest continual mountain uplifts in North America. Most geographers consider the southern limits to lie at Tehachapi Pass south of Bakersfield, where the Sierra merges with the Traverse Ranges of southern California. From its southern terminus, the range stretches northward as a continuous stone wall without any significant gaps or lowlands all the way to Lake Almanor. Here it submerges beneath the volcanic flows of the Cascade Range near Mt. Lassen. But some speculate the

Sierra does not end even there. The lava flows of the Cascade volcanoes may simply hide the range that many geologists believe continues northwest into the Klamath Mountains of northern California.

Although separated from the Sierran block by overlying lava flows and faults, the granites which comprise the Klamath Mountains in northern California and the Peninsula Ranges of southern California and Baja, Mexico, are of similar age and structure to those in the main body of the Sierra Nevada. Therefore, all three mountain uplifts may be part of the same huge mountain range more than 1,500 miles in length, making it among the great mountain ranges in the world! Except for a small splinter group of ridges and peaks by Lake Tahoe (the Carson Range), all of the Sierra Nevada lies in California. Some geologists consider California–Nevada ranges such as the Bodie Hills and

Left: North Peak in the Hoover Wilderness, Inyo National Forest.
Below: Lodgepole pine overlooking Bullfrog Lake in Kings Canyon National Park.

Pine Nut Range to be part of the Sierra Nevada complex as well.

The highest summits are in the southern portion of the range, centered on Mt. Whitney in Sequoia National Park. Here dozens of peaks rise above 13,000 feet, and a few, including Whitney, break the 14,000-foot level. South of Whitney, the most southerly high summit is Olancha Peak that towers 12,123 feet into the sky. After Olancha, the Sierra falls off into a plateau averaging between 9,000 and 7,000 feet, gently rolling south and west towards Tehachapi Pass.

North of Whitney, dozens of high peaks over 13,000 feet rake the sky until another cluster of 14,000-foot summits in the Palisades region west of Big Pine is encountered. Here, six peaks exceed 14,000 feet, including 14,242-foot North Palisade Peak that cradles the Sierra's southernmost glacier, the Palisade Glacier. Between Yosemite National Park on the north and Cottonwood Pass on the south, there are over 500 peaks that exceed 12,000 feet elevation. This 150-mile-long region, largely above timberline, is commonly called the "High Sierra."

As one travels north, the average elevations decrease. Mt. Lyell, at 13,114 feet, is the highest peak in Yosemite National Park. Only a few peaks exceed 10,000 feet in the Lake Tahoe vicinity. By the time you reach the Yuba and Feather River country north of Interstate 80, the average elevation drops to 6,000 to 8,000 feet. The highest summit, Sierra Buttes, tops out at only 8,587 feet.

Because the great length of the Sierra has distinct differences in topography, relief, forest cover, and other characteristics, some geographers divide the range into three sub-units, ignoring the southernmost portions. The High Sierra area stretches from the Kern Plateau to Yosemite National Park, a land dominated by granitic outcrops, alpine tundra and bare jagged peaks. This is the most heavily visited portion of the range. Thousands of lakes set among granite basins lure hikers and climbers into the backcountry.

North of Yosemite to the Tahoe region is what some call the Central Sierra. Though spectacular, it has fewer alpine areas. Much of the granite bedrock is overlain by volcanic rock layers. Only a few large areas of exposed granite exist, such as in the Desolation Wilderness. This region still has its share of granite

lake-studded basins, but the overall relief is lower, with less alpine terrain.

Finally, north of Interstate 80 and Donner Pass, lying in the Yuba River and Feather River basins, is the heavily timbered area of rolling ridges and deep canyons commonly referred to as the Northern Sierra. Some portions of the Feather River Canyon are so steep and wild they are virtually inaccessible. Much of the foothill country of this area is part of the "Mother Lode," and many communities owe their existence to mining operations. This is also the wettest part of the range, and as a consequence, favorable for tree growth. The region has undergone heavy roadbuilding and logging, particularly in the past ten years. Due in part to the greater abundance of private land, it is one of the most developed portions of the range. Communities like Nevada City are experiencing extraordinary growth.

Though trees and minerals have been taken from the mountains for decades, water is the most valuable resource flowing from the Sierra. The 11 major rivers of the range account for nearly half of the runoff in the Golden State. These rivers from south to north are the Kern, Kaweah, Kings, San Joaquin, Merced, Tuolumne, Stanislaus, Mokelumne, American, Yuba and Feather. Without this life-producing water, the Central Valley would look more like the Mojave Desert than the fruitful garden it has become. For example, Bakersfield at the south end of the valley gets little more than 6 inches of precipitation annually. Precipitation increases as one moves northward, to 18 inches at Sacramento. Were it not for the numerous rivers that come brawling out of the snowy Sierra, the extensive development in the Central Valley would not be possible.

A similar reliance upon Sierran east-slope rivers also exists. The Owens River system supplies many of the water needs of the Los Angeles basin, while the Walker, Carson, and Truckee rivers provide water for agricultural interests and cities in northern Nevada.

One can argue that it is the enormous mountain mass of the Sierra Nevada that sets California apart from the rest of the nation, both figuratively and literally. California's mild, genial climate is in part due to the lofty barrier created by the Sierra blocking cold fronts that sweep into the Great Basin from the north and east. Also, the mountains act as sponges that soak up moisture from passing Pacific Ocean

Facing page: Yosemite Falls, at 2,425 feet, is the third-highest falls in the world.

Above: Awananee Hotel in Yosemite National Park.
Top: Thousand Island Lake and Mt. Banner in the Ansel Adams Wilderness.
Left: Octogenarian hikers Jean Nalley and Esta Service in the John Muir Wilderness.

winter storm fronts. The Sierra acts as a giant reservoir, storing snow and providing the thirsty valleys with water during the dry, nearly rainless summers.

Like the Great Wall of China, the Sierra Nevada kept out what the Spanish considered American riffraff. The mountain barrier permitted the Spanish to hold onto their distant California colony with only a few military and mission outposts for perhaps a few decades longer than would have been otherwise possible. The difficulty of travel and access kept most of the fur trappers working rivers farther north and east. In the 1840s, emigrants by the thousands were traveling the "Oregon Trail" to the Pacific Northwest, but most avoided California as their final destination, in part because of the barrier posed by the lofty, rugged Sierra.

It was, however, also these snowy mountains that ended the isolation. In 1848 James Marshall discovered a gold nugget in the tail race at Sutter's Mill on the American River; he set in motion a mass migration to the Golden State that has still not diminished. Nearly every major foothill river in the "Mother Lode" country produced gold in paying quantities. Some were spectacular—the Yuba produced more gold than any other waterway in America. By 1865, this region had given up more than $750 million in gold.

Gold spurred American settlement and quickly fueled the development of agriculture, timber and other resources that were required by the hundreds of thousands of new residents. For a long time after the gold rush era, logging and livestock grazing were important economic activities. Nevertheless, today it is not the resources you can extract and haul away that fuel local economies, but the riches that are more intangible. Extraction industries like logging, grazing and mining are all in steep decline, while recreation and tourism have leaped ahead as the number one economic activities associated with these mountains.

More than 30 million people live within a half day's drive of the Sierra. Recreation and spiritual reconnection to the American landscape dominate the Sierra of today. Mammoth Mountain, for example, gets more skier days of use than any other ski area in the United States. The John Muir Wilderness is the most heavily used designated wilderness in the nation. Out

of the 166 national forests in the country, the Inyo National Forest on the eastern flank of the southern Sierra is fifth in recreation use. The Inyo, the Sierra, Tahoe, and other Sierran national forests account for some 25 million visitor-days—an eighth of all recreation on national forests in the entire nation. In 1991, national forests in the Sierra recorded 31.5 million visitor days—and this figure excludes those who visited national parks, state parks and other tourist destinations.

Although the Sierra of today is under assault from many sources, including smog, excessive logging, subdivisions, and livestock grazing, it is also a place where new beginnings are possible. When the Yosemite Valley was set aside as a state park in 1864, it was the first time the nation protected a piece of land merely for its scenic and spiritual values, the seed from which the concept of our national park system sprouted.

There are now plans and ideas seriously discussed that boldly propose making the entire Sierra a national biological preserve. Such a program would stand as a step forward in our thinking about our relationship to the American landscape. With an ever increasing number of people making California home, it is here that the idea of preserving the biological integrity of ecosystems will be given its ultimate test.

Horse packers along Rafferty Creek, Yosemite National Park. Research by the U.S. Forest Service has shown that the impact of one horse is equal to that of 10 to 25 backpackers.

CLIMATE

The Pacific Ocean significantly influences weather and climate in the Sierra Nevada. Nearly all weather fronts originate over the Pacific, sweep inland, up and over the Sierran wall. There is tremendous variation with elevation and along a south–north gradient. Nevertheless, some generalizations can be made.

The weather in the Sierra Nevada is benign compared to that of many major mountain ranges in the United States, in part because of its southerly position. Tehachapi Pass at the southern part of the range lies at the same latitude as Charlotte, North Carolina and Memphis, Tennessee. The northern end of the range is about the same latitude as Boulder, Colorado, Columbus, Ohio and Philadelphia, Pennsylvania.

Extremes of temperature are rare. Summers are dominated by stable, dry weather, and the winters are snowy, but mild. Major storms do not typically last more than four or five days. It

Below: Snow-covered fir and pine at Lake Tahoe. Ninety-five percent of the precipitation in the Sierra Nevada falls during the winter months.
Right: Shooting star and small tarn by Bishop Pass, where summers are nearly rainless.

Above: Wind-driven "snow banners" fly off Half Dome on a winter day. Yosemite National Park.

Top right: A rosy finch shares peanut butter with hiker Mollie Matteson on top of Mt. Whitney in Sequoia National Park.

Right: Incense cedars in winter along Tenaya Creek, Yosemite National Park. Such mid-elevation areas receive the greatest amount of precipitation.

is not surprising that some have dubbed the Sierra Nevada, a "gentle wilderness."

The characteristic dry summer is due to a high pressure system that usually sits off the coast, bringing clear skies and stable weather. In winter, low pressure systems periodically move south from the Gulf of Alaska, bringing rain and storm fronts to California. As a result, California, and the Sierra Nevada in particular, experience a pronounced wet–dry season. Ninety-five percent of the annual precipitation falls between October and May, with January the wettest month. For instance, January precipitation in Yosemite Valley averages 6.8 inches, while in July the valley receives only .4 inch of moisture with a 97-percent chance of sunshine. Except for an occasional thunderstorm, summers are nearly rainless. That is why some hikers in the Sierra dispense with carrying a tent—a luxury not afforded in most other mountain ranges in the country.

Temperatures over 100 degrees Fahrenheit are common both in the Owens Valley and the Central Valley. The mountain traveler learns that temperatures decrease with elevation. The mean high for Yosemite Valley, at 3,966 feet, is 90 degrees Fahrenheit, with nighttime lows typically in the 50-degree range. By the time you climb to 10,000 feet, maximum temperatures seldom go above 80 degrees, while nighttime temperatures often drop below freezing, even in July.

As temperature *decreases* with elevation, precipitation *increases* up to mid-elevations. For example, in a precipitation/elevation gradient in Sequoia National Park, 20 inches falls at the 2,000-foot level. By the time you reach 7,000 feet, precipitation rises to 55 inches. At 11,000 feet in elevation, annual precipitation drops to 41 inches.

Differences exist between west and east slopes as well. The drop-off in moisture is striking as you cross to the east side of the range. At approximately 5,000 feet on the west slope of the central Sierra, average precipitation is 75 inches annually. The same elevation on the east side typically gets 20 inches. Annual precipita-tion along the main Sierra crest west of Lake Tahoe is about 60 inches. Just slightly east at Mt. Rose in the Carson Range, precipitation drops to 30 inches, while at the foot of the Carson Range in Washoe, Nevada—less than six airline miles from Mt. Rose—annual precipitation is 5 inches or less.

Although the highest mountains are in the southern portion of the Sierra Nevada, more precipitation falls in the northern Sierra. This is caused partly by the gap created in the Coast Range by the Golden Gate strait in San Francisco Bay that permits winter storm tracks to pass uninterrupted to the Sierran wall. Thus, at the 5,000-foot level in Plumas County that lies east of the bay, some 90 inches of annual precipitation falls. In Mariposa County to the south, rainfall is only 55 inches at the same elevation.

Gaps in the mountain barrier also affect local weather. Low passes in the Sierra crest near Mammoth Mountain permit snow-bearing storm fronts to pass to the eastern side of the mountains. Consequently, snowfall is much heavier, with an average of 335 inches of snow per year, explaining why Mammoth Mountain is the site of a major ski resort.

The Sierra also blocks winter cold fronts that funnel south from Canada. Huntington Lake at 6,950 feet in the central Sierra has an average January daytime high of 41 degrees Fahrenheit and a nighttime low of 19 degrees. Compare this with Bridgeport on the eastern slope of the Sierra at nearly the same elevation of 6,400 feet, but with a January average low of 9 degrees. Though the average low is colder, the real difference is found with the record low temperatures. Truckee, California, high on the Sierran east slope near Lake Tahoe, has recorded a low temperature of 30 degrees below zero. Such extremes never occur on the western slope of the range.

In general, the Sierra Nevada has one of the most attractive climates of any mountain range in the United States, which is perhaps the main reason for its popularity as an outdoor recreation destination.

GEOLOGY

The Sierra Nevada is the longest continuous mountain range in the lower 48 states. It is made up of a massive 400-mile-long by 90-mile-wide block of granite tilted up steeply along its eastern margin, with a long, gentle, western grade. Although most people assume that the entire range is a huge granitic outcrop, in reality, only 60 percent of the exposed rock south of Sonora Pass is granitic in origin. North of there, granitic exposures are even fewer, most prominent in the Desolation Wilderness and by Donner Pass.

Volcanic, sedimentary or metamorphic rocks make up the rest of the exposed rock in the range. These rocks often dominate the eastern and western margins, where they rest on the granite buried beneath.

Granitic rocks underlie the entire Sierra, even though the surface outcrops of sedimentary, extrusive volcanic or metamorphic rock may hide the granite. Since surface features are not reliable indicators of sub-surface geological relationships, the geologist's perspective on the

Below: Contact between granite (light colored) and volcanic rock in Granite Chief Wilderness.
Right: Metamorphic rock at Agnew Pass in Ansel Adams Wilderness. Two major metamorphic rock belts straddle the Sierra on both the eastern and western slopes, with granitic rocks sandwiched between.

exact bounds of the Sierra Nevada may be different from the common definition. For instance, rocks of the Sierra Nevada extend beyond the foothills beneath the sediments of the Central Valley. The granites may extend well beyond the normally recognized boundaries of the range as well. Rocks of similar age and kind to those in the Sierra Nevada are found in the Klamath Mountains in northwest California, as well as south into southern California and Baja, Mexico. Geologists speculate that these far-flung ranges may all be part of the same geological complex and thus, technically speaking, all part of the Sierra Nevada.

Large valleys separate the main Sierra crest from the mountains of the Basin and Range Province. These valleys are all structurally related, and defined by faults. Thus the Owens Valley in the south is similar in geological structure to the valleys that enclose Lake Tahoe and the Sierra Valley in the northern Sierra. Nearly all of these valleys, including Owens, Mono, Bridgeport, Tahoe, and Sierra, once held large Pleistocene glacial lakes, but only a few lakes, like Mono and Tahoe, remain.

The gentle western slope of the range is drained by relatively large rivers that have cut deep, spectacular canyons, like those of the Tuolumne, Feather, Kings, and Kern. Rivers on the steep eastern slope, like the Carson, Truckee and Walker, are short, fast, and small. They reflect their recent origins and limited drainage basins that reduce their volume and ability to cut deep canyons.

The present appearance of the range reflects its geological history. The Sierra Nevada is a very young range with a very old history—some of the rocks exposed in the range are more than 450 million years old. Yet it is only in the last 10 million years or so that the Sierra Nevada block began to be uplifted into its present form. Most of the range's rise has occurred in the last 2 million years.

Plate Tectonics

To understand the present range, one must look at plate tectonics theory. According to the theory, the earth is made up of a number of plates that glide or float over the plastic-like inner layer of molten rock known as the mantle. There are two basic kinds of plates: thin, but dense, oceanic rocks; and lighter, but thicker, plates of continental rocks. These plates continuously move about the earth's surface and also change form. Plates can crash together and unite to form mega-continents, or they can tear apart and split, creating micro-plates.

In areas like the Mid-Atlantic Ridge, the sea floor is actually spreading apart. Lava flows out in these spreading zones to create new oceanic basins. As might be expected, since the youngest and newest oceanic rocks occur along the mid-ocean spreading zones, the oldest ocean basin material occurs along the margins, where these ocean basins abut continental plates.

When ocean plates bump into continental plates, they generally dive under the continental plate. Earthquakes or volcanic eruptions are consequences of this collision. As the ocean plate dives deeper under the continental plate, it begins to melt, forming magma (molten rock) that then rises towards the surface, at times burning a hole up through the continental plate's crust. If the magma reaches the surface, it erupts from volcanoes as ash, lava or cinders. If it fails to break through the surface, the magma forms a liquid pool that slowly cools and turns into the crystallized rocks referred to as granite.

Besides creating volcanoes, the collision of plate margins causes mountains to be uplifted, buckled and folded. It is no accident that the world's highest mountains tend to be along the edge of plate margins.

Tectonic History of the Sierra

The Sierra Nevada Range had its beginnings some 400 million years ago, when the western margin of the North American plate was in present-day western Utah. California, Nevada, and most of what is now the western United States did not exist. The shallow ocean that covered the western plate's margin received deep deposits of sediments which eventually solidified into limestone and dolomite. The Snake Range, House Range, Schell Creek Range, and other limestone ranges of eastern Nevada and western Utah are modern-day reflections of this past deposition. Farther west, undersea volcanoes covered the ocean floor with basalt and other volcanic rocks.

Deposition continued in this ocean basin on and off for several hundred million years. Meanwhile, the western margin of the continent gradually moved westward.

During most of this time of deposition, all the large continental plates were united into a large "super continent." About 230 million years ago, this giant continent began to break up into the major land masses we know today. North America broke loose from Europe and Africa and began to move westward, running straight into the Farallon Plate composed of oceanic rocks. As North America continued to drift west, the Farallon Plate was forced beneath it, forming magma that rose towards the surface and solidified into the granite now exposed in the Sierra Nevada.

Water is given off as a by-product of crystallization, and this water often contained metal-rich compounds that formed a molten "soap." These liquids worked up into the overlying metamorphic rocks, and precipitated out silver, lead, copper and gold. These eventually cooled, forming "veins" of quartz rich in minerals. Miners searched for these veins, the "Mother Lode."

Approximately 150 million years ago, the North American plate began to move more rapidly westward. Pieces of the Farallon Plate—mostly sea-floor sediments along with oceanic crust material—were scraped onto the leading edge of the North American continental margin. They formed a mélange, or mixture, of ocean-floor rocks and continental material. These rocks were then severely folded and compressed. The heat and pressure of this plate collision caused the rocks to metamorphose. Sandstone, mudstone, limestone and shale changed into hornfels, phyllite, marble and slate. Volcanic rocks were metamorphosed into schist and graywacke.

Today these metamorphic rocks crop out in numerous places, particularly in the foothill Mother Lode country. Metamorphic rocks are also found along the eastern margin of the range in places such as Ellery Lake just east of Tioga Pass, or in the rocks and contorted marble near Convict Lake. Metamorphic rock that once covered the granitic bedrock still crowns some of the higher peaks. These are called roof pendants, or relict "islands." Examples of peaks capped by roof pendants include Mt. Emerson near Piute Pass, Sierra Buttes, Mt. Dana, Mt. Tallac, and Mt. Morrison.

As the North American plate continued its westward movement, activity in the Sierran region subsided. Erosion began to strip away the overlying rocks and eventually exposed the underlying granitic rocks. The eroded sediments were deposited in the Central Valley. The erosive forces also broke up the gold and silver

veins, and these minerals were transported and concentrated in streams and rivers draining the Sierran foothills. It was this placer gold that precipitated the California gold rush.

As new uplift and volcanic activity occurred, some of the rivers changed course, leaving portions of old stream channels perched above the present river valley. The miners soon learned that these ancient river channels held immense quantities of gold. Using hydraulic water cannons, the gold miners washed away the overlying gravels to expose the gold-bearing layers. This mining technique produced so much sediment that it was outlawed in 1884, but the curious can still see the eroded hillsides of this era at Malakoff Diggins State Park near North Bloomfield.

Volcanic Eruptions

Approximately 30 million years ago, new volcanic eruptions spewed ash and andesite lava over much of the northern Sierra Nevada. Peaks like the Dardanelles, Mt. Rose, Sonora Peak, Levitt Peak and Twin Peaks were all volcanic centers, or are composed primarily of ancient lava flows. These darker volcanic rocks are in obvious contrast to the lighter granites, particularly north of Yosemite. Castle Peak near Donner Pass is a good example of a mountain eroded from these dark andesite lava flows. Other peaks with volcanic origins include Silver Peak, Markleeville Peak, and Highland Peak, all in the Carson–Iceberg Wilderness.

After a period of quiet, volcanic eruptions began again about 10 million years ago. This renewed activity was centered east of the range near present-day Mono Lake and Mammoth Lakes. Volcanic domes, craters, and other features are scattered over the landscape. One 600,000-year-old lava flow in the Middle Fork of the San Joaquin River valley can be seen at Devil's Postpile National Monument. The molten lava cooled into six-sided columns, and glaciers subsequently smoothed the tops of the columns.

About 400,000 years ago Mammoth Mountain began to rise as a giant dome-like volcano. Periodic eruptions have occurred ever since. Geologists would not be surprised if Mammoth Mountain erupted again. A whole string of volcanoes, each successively younger, rise in procession all the way from Mammoth Mountain to Mono Lake, where the newest volcano erupted on the bottom of the lake in 1890. Negit

Above: Spring flowers among granite boulders in the Sierra foothills, Kaweah River, Sequoia National Forest.
Right: Glacially smoothed basalt columns at Devil's Postpile National Monument.
Far right: Domes created by exfoliation of granite at Tenaya Lake in Yosemite National Park.

Above: Glacially carved cirque lakes below Bishop Pass, John Muir Wilderness.
Left: Glacial erratics resting on bedrock at Tenaya Lake, Yosemite National Park.
Top left: Arête carved by glaciers, seen from Mt. Conness, Hoover Wilderness.

Island in Mono Lake is one of the newest volcanoes in the region. The twenty domes of the Mono Craters, composed primarily of obsidian and pumice, form a line of volcanoes just south of Mono Lake. They range in age from 12,000 to 1,800 years. Mono Lake itself occupies a huge, ancient caldera, the collapsed center of a volcano.

Other volcanic outcrops and landscape features include the Volcanic Tablelands running south from Glass Mountain to Bishop. A rain of volcanic ash erupted 700,000 years ago from Glass Mountain. It filled Long Valley with a 500-foot-thick pile of red-hot rhyolitic ash. The ash welded together into "Bishop Tuff." There are excellent views of this tuff along the Sherwin Grade between Bishop and Mammoth.

The fact that molten magma lies not far beneath the surface is evident from the presence of the numerous hot springs lining the edge of the Sierra, particularly in the Mammoth Lakes–Bridgeport region.

Uplift of the Sierra

Sometime about 10 million years ago, the present Sierra Nevada began tilting up along the eastern front, while adjacent crustal blocks sank. The Owens Valley and the Lake Tahoe Basin are both areas where crustal blocks dropped, relative to the rising mountains that cradle them. At first this mountain-building/valley-dropping phase went slowly. It is only in the last one million years that uplift and displacement along faults accelerated, creating the Sierra Nevada as we now know them.

Although it looks like a single fault, the eastern escarpment is really a series of faults along the same axis. Outlying ridges and hills like the Alabama Hills near Lone Pine are composed of the same granitic rocks that make up the Sierra, but they lie between different faults. Uplift has not been as great as with the main crest of the range. Since rivers often seek the line of least resistance, their courses are often determined by past fault structure. The straight and deep Kern River Canyon in the southern Sierra is a fine example of a fault-controlled river channel.

Since this uplift was of a granitic region that had been eroded to a nearly flat surface, much of the present sharp relief is the result of water and glaciers carving deep canyons into the otherwise level tablelands of the Sierra. Remnants of these ancient erosion surfaces are still obvious in places like the Chagoopa Plateau and Boreal Plateau that border the Kern River in Sequoia National Park. Most of the Golden Trout Wilderness with its rolling uplands is a southerly extension of these plateaus. The gentle-sloping summits of many high Sierran peaks like Mt. Whitney, Mt. Langely and others are frequently all that remains of past erosional surfaces.

Recent Glaciation

Probably nothing has done more to shape and define the appearance of the present Sierra than glaciation. Most of the dramatic scenery that draws tourists from around the world has been enhanced or created by the grinding, scouring, and sculpting of these rivers of ice.

Glaciers form when less snow melts than accumulates in summer. Although the climate is often slightly colder during glacial periods, the greatest factor in glacial growth is the increase in cloudy weather and greater precipitation that typically signals the beginning of a glacial period. Over time, the snow turns to ice, and under increasing weight becomes somewhat plastic—like thick toothpaste—and begins to flow.

A glacier does not move randomly over the landscape; it is likely to flow downhill, following the path of least resistance, typically a river valley. As it flows, the land is sculpted. Debris trapped in the bottom of the moving ice acts like a giant file, smoothing the rock surface into a mirror-like surface, leaving scratches called striations. John Muir referred to the striations as the "tracks of glaciers." You can discern the direction and flow of a glacier by these "footprints" left in the rocks.

Imbedded in the ice and carried along the sides are boulders, rocks and gravel. The glacier transports them to its terminus, where they are deposited as the glacier retreats. This heap of unsorted rock left behind is called moraine. Over much of the western slope of the Sierra, the moraines are covered by forests and are difficult for an untrained eye to discern, but on the sage-covered eastern slope, glacial moraines are abundant and easy to spot. Good places to see glacial moraines include the mouths of Convict Lake, June Lake Loop and McGee Canyon by Mammoth Lakes, Bloody Canyon and Lee Vining Canyon by Lee Vining, and Twin Lakes by Bridgeport.

Isolated boulders carried in the glacial ice and left stranded by its retreat are called erratics.

There are numerous places to see such "out of place" rocks: on the sloping granite by Olmsted Point in Yosemite National Park; along the June Lake Loop; and in the Humphrey's Basin by Piute Pass.

As glaciers move down stream valleys, they pluck rock from the sides and flatten the valley bottom, creating a characteristic U-shaped profile. By contrast, water-carved valleys tend to be V-shaped. This difference is easily seen along the Merced River in Yosemite National Park and near Cedar Grove along the Kings River in Kings Canyon National Park. The upper portions of both river valleys are distinctly U-shaped, while the lower reaches are narrower, tighter V-shaped water-carved canyons.

After glaciers retreat, they frequently leave behind truncated side valleys perched high above the main valley. Known as "hanging valleys," these side canyons are points where tributary glaciers joined the main trunk glacier. Since these glaciers drained smaller catchment basins and typically were of a smaller size, they did not scour the valleys as deeply. Once the ice melted, they were left "hanging" higher up the cliff faces. Today, waterfalls commonly emanate from these side valleys, creating such famous features as Yosemite, Bridalveil and Nevada falls. Yosemite Falls, which cascades 2,565 feet, is considered the third-highest falls in the world.

In addition to carving U-shaped valleys, glaciers pluck and grind away at their headwater sources. Here, bowl-like basins called cirques are scoured from rock. Sometimes lakes fill these rocky catchments and are known as cirque lakes, or glacial "tarns" if smaller. The High Sierra is full of these cirque lakes and tarns. The lower elevation of past glaciation can be inferred by the presence of these lakes, since below this region natural lakes are almost nonexistent.

Water trapped behind glacial moraine dams forms lakes. Moraine-dammed lakes include Twin Lakes by Bridgeport; Donner Lake off Interstate 80, Fallen Leaf Lake by South Lake Tahoe; and Convict Lake near Mammoth Lakes.

If several glaciers pluck and grind away at a mountain from opposite sides of a peak, they eventually create knife-edge serrated ridges called arêtes. Sawtooth Peak on the border of Yosemite National Park is a classic example, as is the Ritter Range near Mammoth Lakes. Occasionally, a peak will have cirque glaciers on three or four sides. The glaciers carve a "horn" peak, named for the famous Matterhorn in Switzerland. Cathedral Peak in Yosemite National Park, and Mt. Ritter in the Ansel Adams Wilderness are examples of horns.

The most recent geological event was the Pleistocene Ice Age, which began approximately 3.2 million years ago. A succession of glacial advances and retreats occurred, with the last major advance, the Wisconsin Glaciation, ending only 15,000 years ago. At that time, most of the High Sierra was cloaked in ice up to 4,000 feet thick. An ice sheet 100 miles long and 40 miles wide capped the crest of the range. Only the highest peaks stood above the ice. The summit of Mt. Whitney was one that rose above the ice.

All of the Sierra Nevada Ice Age glaciers disappeared by approximately 10,000 years ago, as the temperatures warmed and the climate became more arid. The small glaciers we see today are the result of renewed glacier formation that accompanied a slight cooling period that reached its height about 1700. Known as the "Little Ice Age," it spawned many glaciers along the Sierran crest. These glaciers often reoccupied the cirques and basins formed during the last major Ice Age. A survey by the U.S. Geological Survey in 1972 counted nearly 500 glaciers in the Sierra. Although most are tiny, the largest, the Palisade, is approximately a mile across. The majority of living glaciers are concentrated in the San Joaquin, Kings and Owens river drainages.

The best places to see existing glaciers include Sawtooth Peak, Conness Peak, Mt. Lyell, and the Kuna Crest in Yosemite; the Ritter Range of the Ansel Adams Wilderness; along the Glacier Divide near Humphrey's Basin; and in the Palisades in the John Muir Wilderness.

HISTORY

The history of the Sierra Nevada reflects past human relationships with the natural landscape throughout the West. There was the long association with the Sierra by native Indian groups, followed by the first contact and exploration by Europeans and Americans. Later, emigrant trails were laid out across the mountain barrier. The trails became highways after 1849 as thousands flocked to scour the foothills for gold. After the gold fever played out, grazing livestock and logging played more prominent roles in the exploitation of the range. At the same time, tourists began to discover the Sierra's beauty and have been coming ever since.

Until very recently most of these human activities focused on taking something away from the mountains—minerals, timber, forage or even recreational experiences. There has been, however, a new trend in thinking that seeks to put something back—restoring ecological pieces and attempting to chart a new course in how people interact with the land. John Muir and other early environmentalists planted the seeds for this change, charting the development of a new land ethic.

Right: Pictographs near Hospital Rock, Sequoia National Park.
Facing page: Former mining town of Bodie on the east side of the Sierra. Gold spurred much of the early development of the Sierra.

Native American Groups

People have been in and around the Sierra for thousands of years. At the time of European contact, the Native American tribes occupying the Sierra Nevada included the Monache, Yokuts, Miwok, and Maidu on the western side of the range. The Washoe and Mono tribes lived along the east slope. Due to the Sierra's deep snow and cold, no tribe actually lived in the higher portions of the range; however, these groups traveled across the Sierra and often spent part of their summers in the cooler, higher elevations.

The Monache were the most southerly of the west slope groups. They occupied the drier southern portions of the Sierra and foothills, including the Kaweah and Kings rivers, in what is now Kings Canyon–Sequoia National Park. These Indians were relatively recent immigrants to the west slope of the Sierra, very likely coming from the Great Basin in only the last five hundred years. In other words, they occupied California at about the same time that the Spanish first came to North America. Unlike most other west slope tribes, the Monache spoke a Shoshonean tongue related to that of the Paiutes who lived in the Owens Valley.

The Yokuts occupied the better locations in the lower foothills and along major rivers in the Central Valley from the Kern River north to the Fresno River. Beyond them, the Miwok ranged north up to the American River, with the Maidu occupying the lands centered on the Feather River country. All were linguistically related to the Penutian language, the dominant tongue of most California tribes.

East of the Sierran crest, the Washoes occupied the Carson Valley and Lake Tahoe region, primarily along the headwaters of the Truckee, Carson and Walker rivers. The Washoe spoke a language derived from the Hokan language family—the only Sierran tribe of this linguistic heritage. South of them were the Monos, a Paiute people, who lived primarily in the Owens Valley and around their namesake, Mono Lake. The language of the Paiutes is related to the Aztec of Mexico and other southwest Shoshonean-speaking peoples.

Because of the mild climate and abundant food resources, the population density of Indians living on the western slope of the Sierra was among the highest in the United States. One estimate is that one of every six Indians in the United States at the time of white contact may have lived within a hundred miles of the Sierra.

Trade between groups was extensive and commonplace. Many of the trails and highways that today cross the Sierra are merely modern upgrades of old Indian travel routes. For centuries, Indians followed a trail up the Dana Fork in Yosemite, over Mono Pass and down Bloody Canyon. Indian trails also crossed Tabosse Pass and Kearsarge Pass to the Kings River, while pathways over Walker Pass led from the Owens Valley to the Kern River. Mono Indians traded obsidian from Glass Mountain, rabbit fur blankets and pinyon nuts for acorns, berries and shells from west slope people.

In comparison to the ecological impacts created by modern society, Indian influences upon the landscape were light. They did, nevertheless, have some effects upon the biological characteristics of these mountains. They hunted and gathered many species of wildlife and plants, and likely caused local extinctions, or at least significant reductions in some species, while enhancing the abundance of others. Native people dug up meadows for roots, and set up traps that often took a good percentage of the fish from a stream. They wore trails into the meadows and trampled forest clearings around their camps. These impacts, however, were local in nature.

Indians also ignited fires to clear out brush and create habitat conducive to some of the wildlife they hunted. They probably set fires accidentally as well. In any event, Indians increased fire frequency in areas where they habitually camped—for example, the Yosemite Valley—and human ignitions as well as other sources like lightning were important in shaping the ecological appearance of the Sierra.

The arrival of Europeans changed Indian cultures permanently. Disease devastated native people and destroyed far more tribes than the U.S. cavalry ever did. While disease was the precursor to cultural destruction, it was the discovery of gold in the Mother Lode country that sealed the fate of the Sierra Nevada tribes. Miners preempted Indian lands, shot game upon which the Indian depended, and polluted rivers with sediments from mining operations. These impacts made it difficult for the Indians to continue their traditional migrations and food-gathering enterprises.

Between 1848 and 1870, some 48,000 Indians—nearly equal to the number of American soldiers who were lost in the Vietnam War—died from disease, starvation and bullets. A few survived and their descendants live in small communities up and down the Sierra.

The Spanish in California

Although Spanish sailors had been plying the coast of California as early as 1542, no inland explorations took place until Gaspar de Portola's party traveled by land from Mexico to San Francisco Bay in 1769. The Spanish built several presidios, or forts, as well as 21 missions in strategic locations from San Diego north to the San Francisco Bay region; however, direct Spanish influence extended little beyond the coast.

The first penetration of the Sierra foothills occurred in 1806, when a Spanish expedition under Gabriel Moraga traveled along the base of the Sierra in the Central Valley. Moraga named several of the features we know today, including the Rio de los Santos Reyes (Kings River), Las Mariposa (Mariposa County), and Rio de Nuestra Senoa de la Merced (Merced River). On another expedition a year later, Moraga traveled across the Sacramento (which he named) and visited the Stanislaus and Mokelumne rivers. This was about the only interest the Spanish expressed in the snowy mountain range that bordered the Central Valley.

Early American Trailblazers

Though the Spanish recorded the existence of the Sierra for the outside world, they did not penetrate the high mountains. It was the American fur trappers who expanded Anglo exploration of the mountains.

The first of these explorer–trappers was Jedediah Smith. Smith came to California in 1826, leading a band of fur trappers from Wyoming via Utah and southern California. In the process, his party became the first Americans to travel overland from the United States to Spanish California. After crossing the Mojave Desert and receiving a cool welcome from Spanish officials in Los Angeles, the trappers made their way north over Tejon Pass into Central Valley. They had a successful winter trapping beaver in rivers flowing from the Sierra. In May 1827, leaving the rest of the party behind to spend the summer in camp along the Stanislaus River, Smith and two companions, Silas Gobel and Robert Evan, set off across the snow-covered mountains to return to Wyoming for supplies. They struggled through deep snow and eventually made a crossing of the range near present day Ebbetts Pass—after losing two horses and a mule to the rigors of the trail.

After a difficult trip across Nevada and Utah, they arrived at the fur trappers' rendezvous in Wyoming at the end of June. By autumn, Smith was back in California. Reunited with the remaining members of his party, Smith traversed north up the Central Valley and into Oregon. Smith had opened the way, and soon other Americans, as well as trappers employed by the Hudson Bay Company of Canada, converged on California. Few, however, ventured into the mountains. In 1833, trapper Joseph Walker led a group eastward across the Sierra from Bridgeport and down the Tuolumne River into what is now Yosemite National Park. They were the first whites to see both Yosemite Valley and Tuolumne Grove of sequoias. After spending the winter trapping Central Valley rivers, Walker and his party left California by a lower and easier route—Walker Pass—which lies near the southern end of the Sierra.

Walker's exploits provided the stimulus for a new group of travelers—the settlers—to take on a crossing of the Sierra. At the time of Walker's journey across the Sierra Nevada in 1833–1834, wagon trains were already moving westward from frontier settlements in Kansas and Missouri to Oregon and California. The first emigrants to travel across the mountain barrier to California were members of the Bartleson–Bidwell Party. After the rugged terrain forced them to abandon their wagons along the West Walker River, they crossed the Sierra in late October of 1841, near Sonora Pass.

A few years later, Charles Fremont, son-in-law of Senator Thomas Hart Benton of Missouri, spent part of several seasons exploring the Sierra, with Joseph Walker and Kit Carson as guides. In 1844, Fremont crossed the Sierra by following the East Fork of the Carson River (near present-day Markleeville) to its headwaters. Then, through deep snows, Fremont and his party struggled over Carson Pass (named for his guide) and managed to reach the headwaters of the American River. They followed the river out to Central Valley. During this floundering passage of the snow-filled range, Fremont climbed Red Lake Peak and spotted Lake Tahoe, becoming the first white person to see

Above: Many Sierra Nevada Indians were migratory, living in seasonal camps in early constructed shelters like this wickiup.
Right: Relic of horse-drawn log cart, Donner State Park. Most of the pine forests around Lake Tahoe were logged by the late 1800s to supply wood and timber for mining camps in Nevada.

Facing page: Early cabin at Pioneer History Center, Yosemite National Park. Steep roofs were designed to shed the heavy snows typical of the Sierra Nevada.

the largest Sierran lake. Fremont eventually returned to the United States via Walker Pass. In late autumn of 1845 he crossed the Sierra again, this time via the Truckee River and Donner Pass. It was Fremont's last major expedition, but he was not done with California. He was later elected a U.S. Senator from The Golden State.

In 1845, an emigrant party under Eliasha Stephen managed with extreme difficulty to cross the Sierra via Donner Pass. Stephen's group became the first wagon party to actually traverse the Sierra Nevada. In the following year, even more emigrants set out from Missouri for sunny California, but one group, known as the Donner party, went down in history. Early snows trapped the party near their namesake lake west of Truckee. By spring when the survivors were rescued, 47 of the 87-member party were dead. Those who lived made it through the winter by eating their dead companions. Today, Interstate 80 follows the emigrant route up the Truckee and over Donner Pass.

In 1851, James Beckwourth, another old-time fur trapper turned guide, scouted out the last major emigrant pass across the Sierra. Beckwourth's Pass, at slightly more than 5,000 feet, is one of the lowest in the entire range. Thousands of emigrants used Beckwourth's Pass to gain access to the Feather River, and from there, on to Central Valley.

Early Mining

The real stimulus for wagon roads came with the discovery of gold. James Marshall found gold at Sutter's Mill on the American River, in 1848. A virtual tidal wave of humanity then descended on California. In 1848 there were 2,000 Americans in all of California. By 1849, there were over 53,000 U.S. citizens, and many more from other lands. Tens of thousands of men and a few women swarmed over the Sierra panning the waterborne gold, or placer deposits, from the gravel in Sierran rivers. By 1852 they had taken gold worth more than $224 million from Sierra streams.

By 1853, giant water cannons were intro-

duced to the Sierra. The cannons washed away entire hillsides, exposing gold buried deep in former river channels. In the 1880s more than 8,000 miles of flumes and ditches carried water to the hydraulic miners. Gold seekers sent millions of cubic yards of dirt and gravel into Sierran streams. Ultimately these tons of sediments wound up in the Sacramento River. The silt raised the river level and caused flooding to such an extent that the practice of hydraulic mining was outlawed in 1884—the first environmental law enacted in California.

Both hydraulic mining and gold panning were used to capture small nuggets and flakes of loose gold mixed in river gravel. This free gold originated in quartz veins known as the Mother Lode. Mining quartz veins required massive capital investments in machinery and equipment; thus only the richest deposits could sustain development. Towns like Nevada City, Grass Valley, Jamestown, and Jackson all owe their existence to the hard rock mines that kept the towns alive long after the loose placer gold deposits played out. A few of these towns, like Jamestown, are reviving as new technology renews interest in the old gold deposits.

The miners wandered widely in the mountains and came increasingly into conflict with Native Americans. In retaliation for an 1851 Indian raid upon a store near Mariposa, a miner named James Savage formed the Mariposa Battalion. Savage and the battalion pursued the offending warriors into the mountains. While some Indians surrendered to the militia, many retreated deep into their mountain stronghold. Following the trail farther up the Merced, the battalion eventually came to the valley known to the Indians as "Yosemite."

Unaware that members of Joseph Walker's party had looked into the same valley during their 1833 crossing of the Sierra, battalion members thought they were the first whites to see the valley. If not the first to view the valley, they were the first to make the wonders of the Yosemite region known to the outside world. By 1855, James Mason Hutchings had brought the first sightseers to visit the valley, thus establishing the tourist trade in the Sierra.

Timber and Livestock

Mining also spurred on at least localized timber production. The abundant forests of the Sierra provided material for housing, mine shaft timbers, and the miles of flumes and diversion dams used in the mining process. When the huge Comstock silver deposits were discovered in Nevada, much of the Tahoe Basin was stripped of timber to provide wood for the growing community.

With the coming of the Central Pacific Railroad, logging took on even greater importance. Saw logs were a major export to the growing cities of the coast and Central Valley. Partially in response to the cut-and-run tactics of these early timber operations, a state forestry board was established in 1883. By the turn of the century, many of the Sierran forests were placed into the newly established National Forest system. Practices on these national forests are still controversial.

The development of the livestock industry went hand in hand with the rush to cut Sierra Nevada forests. Though early explorers repeatedly mentioned the abundance of elk, antelope, and deer in Central Valley, populations of these wild animals declined rapidly in the face of market hunting, and because of lost habitat as the valley's agriculture potential was realized. Ranching quickly began filling the need for fresh meat.

At first most livestock production was concentrated in the foothills and valley bottoms, but drought in the 1860s prompted ranchers to explore the mountains for summer pastures. Sheep were the preferred livestock. Flocks of thousands were driven deep into the mountains by shepherds racing to reach patches of grass before other flocks mowed them clean of forage.

More than any other activity, livestock raising had a severe impact upon the ecological integrity of the Sierra—in part because there were few parts of the range where sheep were not herded. Sheep hooves trampled the soils. Voracious appetites drove sheep to strip meadow after meadow of all vegetation. Sheepherders regularly killed native predators like the mountain lion and grizzly; disease transmitted from the domestic sheep to wild sheep was a primary factor in the demise of the Sierra's native bighorns.

Whitney Surveys

Although many miners, stockmen, and hunters had penetrated the Sierra, few brought back written reports or maps. In 1860, the California Legislature established a state Geological Survey to determine the location and value of the state's mineral resources, as well as to compile information regarding the state's botanical and zoological riches. Heading up the survey was Josiah Dwight Whitney (for whom Mt. Whitney is named). William Brewer was his assistant in charge of field surveys. Other survey members included Clarence King and Charles Hoffmann.

During the summer of 1863, the Whitney survey party investigated the Yosemite region. They explored the Yosemite Valley, and then moved to the high country and climbed the peak now named for Hoffmann. As the summer progressed, the survey party explored the Tuolumne Meadows area. They eventually worked northward toward Lake Tahoe, exploring much of the country in between.

In 1864, the survey was focused on the southern Sierra Nevada, one of the least known portions of the state—the high Sierra near the head of the Kern, Kings and Kaweah rivers. They worked east through the Big Trees in what is now Sequoia National Park, and climbed and named Mt. Silliman. Seeing rugged peaks to the east, they trudged deeper into the mountains, crossed Roaring River, and climbed Mt. Brewer, named for William Brewer. The party saw still higher peaks on the horizon, which they named Williamson, Whitney and Tyndall—all three taller than 14,000 feet and among the highest peaks in the range. King and Cotter (a packer hired for the summer) left the rest of the party to climb these high peaks; they successfully ascended Tyndall, but did not make it to the top of Whitney.

During the summer, the Brewer party encountered a group of miners on the trail between Big Meadows and Kings Canyon. The miners had come from the Owens Valley and included Thomas Keough (for whom Keough Hot Springs is named) and John Bubbs (for whom Bubbs Creek in Kings Canyon is named). With the miners as guides, the Brewer party explored the magnificent Kings Canyon. That summer they named the Palisades, Mt. Goddard, and other peaks. Eventually, they made their way to the Owens Valley via Kearsarge Pass. After reaching the Owens valley, the Whitney survey party moved north to Rock Creek, up over Mono Pass, down to the Vermilion Valley, and eventually northward back to Yosemite to finish their summer's work.

The survey had traversed most of the high country in the Sierra, establishing its bounds and naming many of its most prominent features. Although the survey placed names on the map, the party had not passed through unexplored country. Even as they crossed the southern Sierra, they met miners traveling from the Owens Valley to the Central Valley. While Brewer was on Mt. Gibbs in Yosemite, he mentioned seeing tourists on the summit of nearby Mt. Dana.

John Muir and the Conservation Movement

By the 1860s tourists were already flocking to Yosemite; more and more of the valley was developed and privatized. Concern arose that the public might eventually find itself locked out of the landscape that it owned. In response, Senator John Conness introduced a bill into Congress in 1864 requesting that federal land in the Yosemite Valley and Mariposa sequoia grove be given to California for protection as a park.

This was a landmark achievement. It signaled the first steps in a change of official government policy that was until then, and for a long time thereafter, to actively to dispose of all its lands into private hands. Setting aside *any* parcel for public enjoyment and protection of scenic and natural values represented a radical departure from the policy of the day. Yosemite State Park was created eight years before Yellowstone National Park, thus setting the stage for Yellowstone's protection, and establishing a model for the national park system.

To the newly established park came a young midwesterner who would forever be associated with the valley and the Sierra. His name was John Muir. Muir was born in Scotland, raised on a stump farm in Wisconsin, and arrived in California in 1868, after a thousand-mile walk from Wisconsin to Florida. During his first ten years in California, he lived year-round in the Sierra, gaining an intimacy with this range that few have matched since. Muir's relationship to the mountains was spiritual. Many who would later accompany him in the high country thought the slim, bearded, clear-eyed Muir bore a striking resemblance to Jesus, and certainly his exuberant "sermons" on wilderness only added to that impression.

In addition to his messianic fervor, Muir also possessed a great scientific mind. He was one of the first to work out many of the early principles of Sierran glacial history. Gravitating to the Yosemite Valley shortly after his first glimpse of the Sierra in 1868, Muir spent his first season herding sheep in the high country of Yosemite. The remainder of the fall and winter he operated a sawmill in the Yosemite Valley for an innkeeper.

In between bouts of employment, there was plenty of time for explorations of the valley. Muir, through careful observation, gradually came to believe that glaciers had shaped many of the spectacular features of the Yosemite region, from the hanging waterfalls to the smoothed domes of the high country.

Muir's theories contradicted those of most prominent geologists of the day, who thought the Yosemite Valley was formed by a great catastrophic event. The strongest proponent of this view was Josiah Whitney, head of the California Geological Survey. Whitney saw Muir as an uneducated upstart and denigrated his glaciation theories as nothing more than the insane babbling of an "ignorant sheepherder."

In the summer of 1869, however, Muir met Joseph LeConte, a professor of geology from the University of California. Together they wandered through the high country, camped at Tenaya Lake and climbed Mt. Dana, all the while discussing Muir's theories about glaciers. In LeConte, Muir found a sympathetic ear. Soon LeConte was joining Muir as a proponent of the glaciation theory.

Other scientists began flocking to Muir's small cabin, and wandering the high country listening to his explanations. In 1871, the presi-

Below: Active mining on the North Fork Feather River.
Right: Old steam engine and stamp mill, Plumas Eureka State Park. Gold was scattered throughout the Sierra, but the greatest extraction occurred in the northern sections.

dent of Massachusetts Institute of Technology (MIT) visited Muir and urged him to publish his ideas. Later that fall, Muir sent an article, "Yosemite Glaciers," to the *New York Daily Tribune*, establishing his claim as the first to explain glaciers as the agent that shaped the Yosemite landscape. Subsequent research would demonstrate that Muir placed too much emphasis upon glaciers as an explanation for Yosemite Valley features, but his interpretations and views were still ahead of his time.

In 1872, Muir discovered living glaciers near Mt. McClure in Yosemite and brought LeConte to see them. LeConte then published a paper on Yosemite's glaciers, giving Muir full credit as well as a much-needed confirmation of his theories.

Searching for even more evidence to support his geological studies and theories, Muir made several treks south of Yosemite. In 1873,

and again in 1875, he roamed as far as the Kings River, where he made the first ascent of Mt. Whitney from its cliff-like eastern side.

Muir had a universal curiosity and was as interested in the trees and flowers as in the rocks upon which they grew. During his last major trip to the southern Sierra, in 1875, Muir patiently explored all of the sequoia groves he could locate, attempting to map their distribution and define their basic ecology. He wandered for days in the grand forests that lay between the Middle and Marble forks of the Kaweah. These he named the "Giant Forest"— now part of Sequoia National Park. South of there, in the Tule River drainage, he found loggers already whittling away at the giant trees. It proved to be a turning point in his life.

In his journal, Muir mused, "Will man cut down all the forests to build ships and houses? Will all the alpine gardens become sheep and cattle pastures and be grazed and trampled to death?" The following year, Muir sounded the first call for protecting the giant sequoia forests in an article called "God's First Temples: How Shall We Preserve Our Forests?" This piece signaled the beginning of his life's calling. After his 1875 trip, he gave up science to champion conservation efforts.

In 1880, Muir married Louise Wander Strentzel, whose father was a prosperous horticulturist in California. They settled down to a domestic life of tending the farm. Although Muir made a few trips, he did little writing or wilderness roaming for nearly ten years. Then, in 1889, he met Robert Underwood Johnson, editor of the influential *Century Magazine*. Together they set out for a camping trip in Yosemite. After wandering through Tuolumne Meadows that had recently been ravaged by sheep, Muir launched into a diatribe against livestock grazing.

Prompted by the visible effects of the livestock, Johnson urged Muir to begin a campaign for the creation of a Yosemite National Park. Park establishment would mandate livestock removal to protect the watersheds of the Sierra. Johnson pledged to help the cause by publishing Muir's accounts in *Century Magazine*. The following summer, two articles, "The Treasures of Yosemite" and "Features of the Proposed National Park," appeared in *Century Magazine*. Muir proposed that the entire watersheds of the Merced and Tuolumne rivers be protected as national

President Teddy Roosevelt (left) spent four days with John Muir in Yosemite National Park. Muir influenced Roosevelt's establishment of several national parks and an expansion of Yosemite in 1905.

YOSEMITE NATIONAL PARK RESEARCH LIBRARY

Left: Before 1913, horse and stage travel provided the only access into Yosemite National Park.

Below: Stoneman House beneath Half Dome in 1880, Yosemite National Park. Unchecked development that threatened to overrun the valley prompted conservationists like John Muir to pressure for federal control of Yosemite Valley.

park. The response was immediate and overwhelming. By late summer a bill that essentially followed Muir's recommendations was introduced into Congress, debated, and swiftly passed into law on October 1, 1890. Since the Yosemite Valley was already protected as a state park, it was, for the time being, not part of Yosemite National Park.

Parks in the Southern Sierra

While public scrutiny had focused on Yosemite, efforts were underway to protect portions of the southern Sierra as well. George Stewart, editor of the *Visalia Delta*, lobbied endlessly for protection of the sequoias and mountains along the headwaters of the Kaweah, Kern and Kings rivers. Arguing that logging and grazing threatened the watersheds which valley farmers depended upon, Stewart galvanized local support for land protection.

To understand part of the urgency Stewart, Muir and others felt, one must remember that at this time, without designation as national park, there was no way to preclude settlers, timber cutting, or livestock grazing.

To preempt loss of public ownership, individuals and groups as early as 1881 proposed a Sierra Nevada alpine national park for the region around Mt. Whitney and the Upper Kern drainage. In that same year, U.S. Senator John Miller from California introduced a bill to protect a huge tract of land in the southern Sierra, largely taking in what is today Kings

CALIFORNIA STATE LIBRARY PHOTOS

Canyon–Sequoia National Parks. The bill, too ambitious for the times, died without action; however, efforts to preserve some of the southern Sierra did not end. Stewart continued to promote the need for a national park for the region.

In 1890, Stewart's efforts were rewarded. Within the Yosemite Park bill were the seeds of two other national parks. A small subsection of the Yosemite act withdrew federal lands for new national parks in the southern Sierra around the General Grant Grove and the Giant Forest—General Grant National Park and Sequoia National Park.

Almost immediately there were calls to enlarge these parks. In 1890, John Muir mailed Robert Johnson a map delineating boundaries he had drawn for an enlarged Sequoia National Park, encompassing all the sequoia groves from the Kings River Canyon south to the Tule River, and the High Sierra as far east as Mt. Whitney. The following summer, Muir published a piece in *Century Magazine* promoting preservation of Kings Canyon. In "A Rival of the Yosemite," Muir publicly outlined his proposed expansion of Sequoia National Park.

Until 1891, the only means of protecting the land from logging and grazing, or being sold into private ownership, was to create a national park. A new mechanism was created when President Benjamin Harrison signed into law a bill that defined a system of national forest reserves. These reserves could be established by presidential decree. The reserves permanently withdrew lands from sale under the Timber and Stone Act and other federal laws. Nearly as soon as the bill was passed, Robert Johnson advocated that all of the Sierra Nevada be placed in a huge forest reserve.

Prompted by Muir's article and the publicity it aroused, and by Johnson's lobbying efforts, President Harrison created the four-million-acre Sierra Forest Reserve in 1893. The reserve stretched from Yosemite south to the Kern River. Harrison also created fourteen other reserves throughout the West, setting aside millions of acres from entry and private acquisition. The following year, newly-elected President Grover Cleveland added millions more acres to the system. At the time, there was not much difference between a national park or national forest reserve. Mining, logging and grazing were all forbidden in both forest reserves and parks.

Western extractive interests were well-represented in Congress. They lobbied ceaselessly for changes in regulations, and even introduced a bill into Congress to dismantle the forest reserve system.

Gifford Pinchot, who became the first director of the U.S. Forest Service, joined Muir to head off the loss of the Forest Reserves. Pinchot was later to battle John Muir over damming Hetch Hetchy Canyon in Yosemite. Pinchot believed regulated timber harvest and grazing, based upon scientific principles, should be permitted on public lands. Though not preservation-oriented, Pinchot's philosophy was, nevertheless, a radical departure from the standard cut-and-run and overgrazing practices that typified most western resource policies. A ceaseless promoter of this concept, Pinchot found favor with President Theodore Roosevelt. Roosevelt not only designated many more forest reserves in the West, but supported the creation of a U.S. Forest Service (1905) to administer these lands, with Pinchot as its first director.

Millions of acres were withdrawn from entry as part of the National Forest Reserve system, but there were no mechanisms for administering them until 1897. With western grazing interests leading the charge, forest policies were drawn up which permitted grazing, as well as logging and mining, on forest reserve lands.

These changes brought about a split between Muir and Pinchot. Muir favored a total ban on livestock use of forest reserves, saying: "fire and pasturage chiefly threaten the reserve forest lands of the public domain. In comparison with these, the damage that is inflicted on them by illegal timber cutting is insignificant." Muir actually advocated placing armed guards in the mountains to enforce the grazing ban; he suggested, "One soldier in the woods, armed with authority and a gun, would be more effective in the forest preservation than millions of forbidding notices."

Pinchot, on the other hand, felt he needed to accommodate the livestock interests if forest reserves were to survive the onslaught of Western parochial interests. While agreeing with Muir about the damage incurred by livestock grazing, he advocated regulated use. This divergence in philosophy lead to a division within the growing conservation movement. "Wise use" proponents like Pinchot were eventually denounced by John Muir.

Facing page, top: Family tombstone at Manzanar World War II internment camp in the Owens Valley. Ten camps in five states held 100,000 Americans citizens of Japanese descent. More than 10,000 were held at Manzanar. Manzanar National Historic Site.
Bottom: A street in modern Sierra City, a former gold-mining town, in northern California.

This split represented a difference in basic philosophy. Muir argued against a human-centered view. He denounced those who considered all things alive or dead as "resources" for human consumption. "The world, we are told, was made especially for man—a presumption not supported by all the facts. A numerous class of men are painfully astonished whenever they find anything, living or dead in all God's universe, which they cannot eat or render in some way what they call useful to themselves." Muir believed that the land and its wild inhabitants had inherent rights in and of themselves, and this would put him increasingly at odds with the utilitarian concepts advocated by Pinchot.

To provide a voice for conservation ideas, Muir and 27 other Sierra Nevada advocates formed the Sierra Club in 1892. Muir was elected president, a post he held for 22 years until his death. One of the first successful campaigns led by the Sierra Club was the transfer of Yosemite Valley back into federal ownership in order to counter what many conservationists felt was the state's lack of responsible administration and the threat of growing privatization of the area.

In this effort Muir was aided by the president of the United States. In 1903, Theodore Roosevelt visited Muir for four days in Yosemite. They camped out and discussed conservation issues and the need to create additional national parks throughout the country. With Roosevelt's approval, Yosemite Valley was transferred back to federal ownership and incorporated into Yosemite National Park in 1905.

The Battle for Hetch Hetchy

Shortly after the giant earthquake of 1906, San Francisco applied to the Secretary of Interior for permission to build a dam and water storage reservoir in Hetch Hetchy Canyon on the Tuolumne River. Muir often compared Hetch Hetchy with the Yosemite Valley in terms of beauty and grandeur, and he adamantly opposed the project. When the dam application was approved by Secretary of Interior Garfield in 1908 based upon the argument that domestic water use outweighed wilderness preservation, Muir and the Sierra Club launched a nationwide campaign to stop it.

Muir wrote to President Roosevelt suggesting that alternative dam sites outside of "our wild mountain parks" could supply San Francisco's needs. In Roosevelt, Muir had a

sympathetic ear; however, Garfield reported to Roosevelt that no suitable alternative existed. In addition, Roosevelt's close friend Gifford Pinchot was among the dam supporters. Reluctantly, Roosevelt went along with granting the dam permit.

Muir labeled his foes "temple destroyers" and scornfully declared, "Dam Hetch Hetchy! As well dam for water tanks the people's cathedrals and churches, for no holier temple has ever been consecrated by the heart of man."

Although Roosevelt generally supported Pinchot, the president's discomfort with defiling a wild place eventually caused him to retreat from his earlier endorsement of the proposed dam. By the time the permit application came up for a vote in Congress, however, Roosevelt was no longer president. In the end, despite the national outcry in support of preserving the park, dam proponents won. The Senate voted to approve the permit and President Woodrow Wilson signed the bill on December 19, 1913.

Although Muir was dejected by his failure to save Hetch Hetchy, the campaign did signal a success for him in some ways. The fact that a national dialogue had occurred, which discussed preservation of some distant valley, was in itself an expression of changing American attitudes towards wilderness. Wildlands were no longer places to be developed as swiftly as possible. Instead, many people saw a value in keeping some parcels of the American landscape in a natural condition—perhaps not nearly as much value as providing a water supply to a large urban area, but enough to argue about it.

Enlargement of Southern Sierra Parks

The loss of the Hetch Hetchy dam fight only increased the anxiety of those committed to protecting the Sierra. New proposals for enlargement of Sequoia National Park were formulated.

In 1911 conservationists recommended that all of the Kern and Kings rivers watersheds (basically the outline of today's Kings and Sequoia National Parks) be incorporated into Sequoia National Park. Senator Frank Flint of California introduced such a bill to Congress. Livestock interests, however, successfully lobbied to stop the bill.

During the presidency of Calvin Coolidge, a compromise designated park protection for the southern portion of the Sierra south of the Kings–Kern Divide, leaving out the Kings River

Early-day tourists in Yosemite National Park.

drainage. With almost no opposition in Congress, the bill passed and was signed into law on July 3, 1926.

Despite the passage of the Sequoia National Park expansion, proponents for the Kings River Canyon continued to lobby for park protection of that region. In 1935, Secretary of Interior Harold Ickes publicly supported a proposal to make a John Muir–Kings Canyon wilderness national park. Opposition at this point came mostly from irrigation interests in the San Joaquin Valley who wanted the option of constructing storage reservoirs at several Kings Canyon sites. Nevertheless, several bills were introduced into Congress, and after much wrangling, Congress approved creation of a 450,000-acre Kings Canyon National Park. President Franklin Roosevelt signed it into law on March 4, 1940. In 1965, small additions at both Cedar Grove and Tehipite Valley were added to the existing Kings Canyon National Park.

Roads Across the Sierra

In their early years, both the Park Service and the Sierra Club were advocates of more road access to the mountains. Indeed, John Muir believed that people needed to see the mountains if they were to protect them from logging, grazing and mining. This policy, however, began to change by the 1920s as the fledgling wilderness movement grew. There was no shortage of road proposals, but in most cases, high construction costs and potentially limited seasonal use kept proposals tabled. Nevertheless, a few of the schemes got more than passing attention. One of the most ambitious was "The Sierra Way," which proposed to link Lake Isabella on the Kern River with Yosemite National Park on the north. Later this was lengthened to include the high country north, all the way to Mt. Shasta.

Almost immediate opposition to the proposed highway developed from those who wanted to keep the High Sierra roadless and wild. Some of the staunchest opposition came from the Park Service and Sierra Club, both of which were increasingly supportive of wilderness protection. Their lobbying efforts paid off, and plans for The Sierra Way were dropped. That did not, however, stop people from dreaming of other trans-Sierra roads. One road was to run up Kings Canyon and over Kearsarge Pass to Independence in the Owens Valley. Another would have run from Hockett Meadow to Lone Pine,

across what is now the Golden Trout Wilderness. A third proposed road would have crossed the Sierra from Mammoth Lakes to the San Joaquin Valley. Wilderness and park designation have precluded construction of all these roads.

Today, the 250-mile parcel of Sierra high-country from the Sherman Pass Highway on the south, to the Tioga Pass road in Yosemite, is the longest stretch of undeveloped and roadless wildlands left in the lower 48 states.

Owens Valley Water Wars

The Los Angeles Basin has a mild climate year-round, dramatic scenery, and access to a variety of landscapes. It was a city destined to greatness if it had just one more ingredient— water. Just after the turn of the century, realizing that lack of water might limit growth, the city began to look for new sources. They found it in the Owens River Valley on the east side of the Sierra. At this time, the federal government was considering making the Owens Valley an example of desert reclamation, with plans to develop irrigation canals to create 60,000 acres of new agricultural fields in the basin. This would have hastened the development and transfer of public lands into the private sector, by subsidizing irrigation water for farmers.

These reclamation plans were never realized. In 1903, Los Angeles secretly bought up strategic water rights and ranches up and down the Owens Valley, and laid plans for construction of a 233-mile aqueduct. There were tales of illegal, or at least shady, real estate deals by individuals associated with the various water acquisitions. None of these claims prevented Los Angeles from getting its water and aqueduct.

After more water rights were bought in the 1920s, valley residents revolted. They dynamited the aqueduct and staged protests that brought nationwide recognition to the Owens Valley. Los Angeles was forced to send a trainload of armed detectives to guard the water supplies. Tensions remained high for nearly a decade; however, many of the valley's remaining ranch families moved out during the drought years of the 1930s.

There may be a positive side to Los Angeles's transfer of water. Had it not occurred, the newly created Reclamation Service may have done the same kind of dewatering and river-damming as the city. Furthermore, public lands still undeveloped today may have been transferred into private hands.

MONO LAKE

Mono Lake lies at the foot of the Sierra near Lee Vining, just east of Yosemite National Park. It is one of the oldest continuously existing bodies of water in North America. Geologists speculate it may be more than 700,000 years old. It was considerably larger when Ice Age glaciers fed its waters—the lake was nearly 60 times its present size.

Mono Lake owes its existence to two forces: the glaciers that flooded its basin; and volcanoes which are still reshaping its shorelines. Two of the lake's islands—Negit and Paoha—are volcanic islands that only appeared 1,700 and 325 years ago, respectively.

With no outlet, Mono Lake, like Great Salt Lake, is gradually accumulating salts from inflowing streams. These salts make its waters unsuitable for fish. Nevertheless, the lake is a biological treasure. Tiny freshwater shrimp and brine flies sustain dozens of different bird species. As many as 140,000 phalaropes and 750,000 eared grebes may stop over here to "refuel" during migration. And between 85 and 90 percent of the Golden State's entire population of California gulls nest on islands within Mono Lake.

Since 1941, the Los Angeles Water Department has been diverting water from creeks that flow into Mono Lake. As a consequence, the lake has fallen more than 40 feet, the volume has dropped by half, and the salinity has increased. In 1978, fearing that the Mono could become unsuitable for wildlife, or perhaps even disappear altogether, local conservationists formed the Mono Lake Committee to lobby for protection of the lake.

In 1984, Congress declared the lake and surrounding lands a National Forest Scenic Area and mandated that the ecological and scenic values of the area be maintained and preserved. In addition, since the changing salinity of the lake threatened Mono's unique brine shrimp with extinction, the Fish and Wildlife Service proposed listing the species under the Endangered Species Act.

In 1983, the Audubon Society filed suit against the Los Angeles Water Department, arguing that the public trust doctrine required that Mono Lake be protected. In 1991, the California Supreme Court concurred and ordered the Los Angeles Water Department to maintain sufficient water in Mono Lake tributary streams to sustain the lake ecosystem.

Dawn in Mono Lake Scenic Area, Inyo National Forest. The porous limestone (tufa) columns were formed from calcium carbonate deposited by underground springs; they were exposed as water was diverted from the lake.

Manzanar

Another disgraceful part of American history was also played out in the Owens Valley. The Manzanar internment camp was established near Lone Pine in 1942. Thousands of American citizens of Japanese ancestry were imprisoned—without trial or being accused of anything other than being of Japanese descent. They were taken away from their jobs, homes, and sometimes even their families, and forced to live in drafty, wooden tarpaper shacks beneath the Sierra. Surrounded by barbed wire and guard towers, as many as 10,000 Americans were locked behind Manzanar's gates. Ironically, some of their relatives were fighting in both Europe and the Pacific to "keep freedom alive." The camp was closed in 1945 and the prisoners released.

Today one can see a few ruins located off of Highway 395. In 1992, the federal government named Manzanar a national historic site to commemorate a tragic period in American history.

Fight over Mineral King

The last major conservation controversy in the southern Sierra came in the 1970s in a remote mountain valley named Mineral King.

This peaceful valley belies its tumultuous history. Site of a short-lived mining boom in the late 1800s, Mineral King later became a summer home area for residents of the San Joaquin Valley. Because of its past mining history, the area was not included in Sequoia National Park, although the park surrounded the basin on three sides. In 1965, Walt Disney unveiled plans for construction of a massive ski resort in this charming valley.

When Disney's plans for development of the basin were announced, the Sierra Club immediately began a campaign to stop the resort. In 1969, the club took the Forest Service and Disney Corporation to court. The case went all the way to the U.S. Supreme Court.

There were a number of reasons conservationists opposed the resort. The developers envisioned a world-class ski area with 22 lifts, 16 restaurants, 1,200 cabins, condominiums, 2.5 million visitor days a year, and 3,600 vehicles a day. To sweeten the pot, the state promised to subsidize a high-speed highway that would have bisected national park lands for miles. The Forest Service, faced with five development alternatives for the proposed resort, chose maximum development in its Final Environmental Statement.

Below: Early tourists to Yosemite frequently stayed in cotton wall tents.

Facing page, top: Horseback excursion party below Yosemite Falls, 1870.
Bottom: Early mining community of Bennettville.

CALIFORNIA STATE LIBRARY

By then, however, the Sierra Club was in high gear. Members lobbied Congress and the developers through the press, and even staged a protest at Disneyland in 1973. Due to growing opposition, the state withdrew its funding for the proposed highway. By 1975, the economic attractiveness of the proposal had declined significantly, and Disney Corporation withdrew its plans. Shortly thereafter legislation that called for the transfer of Mineral King from the Forest Service to the Park Service passed Congress, and in 1978 President Jimmy Carter signed the bill, making Mineral King part of Sequoia National Park.

Wilderness Battles

The Wilderness Act passed Congress in 1964. The purpose of the act was to provide a mechanism to preserve undeveloped land and the wildlands resource for "future generations," by prohibiting development and incompatible uses such as motorized access. Areas given immediate protection under the act include the John Muir Wilderness, the Minarets Wilderness (now Ansel Adams Wilderness) and Hoover Wilderness. Despite this start, there were some large tracts of roadless lands in the Sierra, like Mineral King, that lacked any kind of protection against logging, mining, and recreational development. Working continuously, groups like the California Wilderness Coalition, Sierra Club and Wilderness Society successfully guided the California Wilderness Act through Congress in 1984. This act added 3.2 million acres to the Wilderness System statewide, including nine new areas in the Sierra, as well as most of the backcountry in Sequoia, Kings Canyon and Yosemite. Today, these Sierra Nevada wildlands make up the second largest roadless complex in the contiguous 48 states, with only the Central Idaho Wildlands larger.

Despite these past successes, new concerns over dangers to the ecosystem from logging have prompted conservationists to request the addition of 400,000 acres to Sequoia National Park. Others are calling for a Range of Light National Park to take in the Sierra from Yosemite to Kernville. An even more ambitious idea is to make the range a biological preserve. These proposals reflect the increasing concern for protection of entire biological communities, in areas large enough to preserve ecological processes and functions.

CALIFORNIA STATE LIBRARY

YOSEMITE NATIONAL PARK RESEARCH LIBRARY

45

PLANT LIFE

A diversity of habitats, and thus, a large
number of species, are found in the immense
width and length of the Sierra Nevada. The
Sierran forest sustains 25 species of conifer and
41 species of hardwood. A similar diversity of
shrubs exists. Only the alpine flora is more
limited than in other areas. For instance, in
Yosemite National Park (which represents only
a small portion of the Sierra's western slope),
more than 1,400 species of shrubs, trees and
flowering plants have been recorded. Few parts
of the United States can boast greater plant
diversity than the Sierra.

Below: Rock fringe in
crevice at Siberian Pass,
Sequoia National Park.
Right: Blue oak and
poppies in the Sierra
foothills near Pinehurst.

The major plant communities or associations found in the Sierra differ by aspect, slope, elevation and side of the mountain range. For instance, pinyon pine, a species common on the east side of the range, is seldom found west of the main crest. On the other hand, black oak is a west-slope species that only occurs in a few well-watered east-side canyons. Even within the same general area, north slopes that lie in the shade most of the day are wetter and cooler than south slopes. Thus, at the same elevation, one side of a river canyon might be covered with Douglas-fir forest, while the opposing sunny slope may have grasslands or chaparral. The plant associations usually found at higher elevations in the south occur lower in elevation as one moves north.

Several factors influencing plant distribution include soil properties, water availability, temperatures, frost tolerance, presence of mycorrhizal fungi, snow cover, available sunlight, and adaptations to disturbances such as fire. As the variables change, so do the plants growing on a particular site. For example, immediately after a fire and in the absence of forest cover, a slope may be hot and dry. Grasses and shrubs tolerant of hot, dry conditions may invade the site. Over time, however, their shade enables species that prefer cooler, moister conditions to gain a foothold. Eventually, the shade species may come to dominate the site. This process is called succession; the species finally dominating the site are known as climax species.

The changes continue until the climax condition is reached. Change stops and the same species reproduces repeatedly on the site. Thus, without fire, shade-tolerant white fir will eventually shade out young ponderosa pine that require full or nearly full sunlight to maintain vigor. Over time, fir will replace pine on the site. With these qualifiers in mind, there are some generalizations that can be made.

Oak–Digger Pine Woodland Zone

Beginning with the west slope, the plant community lowest in elevation is the grassland–oak–digger pine zone. It is found as low as 500 feet in the north, and up to 5,000 feet in the south. This is the beautiful "Mother Lode" oak woodland country of the foothills. Grasses, predominantly non-native annuals introduced from Eurasia, such as red brome, soft chess, and wild oat, dominate the foothills. The original native grassland species, mostly perennial bunchgrasses, are now largely gone due to overgrazing by livestock and to agricultural development. Relict populations occur in isolated, ungrazed, unplowed regions.

Scattered savanna-like stands of digger pine, interior live oak, and blue oak grow in the foothills. Digger pine is easily identified by its lacy, 8- to 10-inch long, gray-green foliage and large, scaly, four-pound cones. Interior live oak has dark, leathery evergreen leaves. This tree forms picturesque woodlands in the foothills. Blue oak is deciduous, with barren branches in winter. It is so well adapted to its arid habitat that it gradually dies if more water is made available to it.

Numerous wildflowers adorn this zone in the spring, including purple owl's clover, larkspur, paintbrush, California poppy, lupine, meadowfoam, prettyface, popcorn flower, common madia, and baby blue eyes. Along streams one encounters California buckeye and the lovely redbud.

Chaparral Zone

On drier, hot, thin-soil sites throughout the foothills and lower forest zone, there are dense thickets of evergreen shrubs known as chaparral, Spanish for "scrub oak." The associated species include whiteleaf manzanita, buckbrush, and scrub oak. These species are typically three to six feet in height, although on well-watered sites, some chaparral plants can approach the size of small trees. Canyon oak, often a component of the chaparral zone, is abundant on the cliffs in the Yosemite Valley. At times, it will attain a height of 25 feet, with a trunk up to a foot in diameter.

This vegetation type is one of the most flammable plant communities in the West. Many chaparral species actually contain volatile oils that increase their flammability. Burning might seem like a poor survival strategy, but for the chaparral it is an advantage. Most chaparral species would be replaced by woodlands if periodic fires did not remove the trees. Since most chaparral species sprout from their roots, they can immediately recolonize the site, using the existing root system to provide both water and nutrients—a distinct advantage over competing plant species. In addition to sprouting, most chaparral species also mature early and can readily reseed a site, and they produce fire-resistant seeds. In fact, the seeds of some manzanita and ceanothus species will not even germinate without heat from a fire.

Sierran Mixed Conifer Forest Zone

The Sierran mixed conifer forest is found at elevations as low as 1,200 feet in the north and at elevations as high as 10,000 feet in the south. Generally, growth is best between 3,000 and 7,000 feet elevation. This is the true forest zone of the Sierra—the zone where the majority of timber harvests have occurred. Depending upon slope, aspect and elevation, different species dominate.

The lowest elevations tend to be occupied by ponderosa pine. Thick, scaly, yellow bark and needle bundles in groups of three identify this tree. (The similar Jeffrey pine dominates east-slope forests and higher elevations of the west slope.) The thick bark and branch-free columnar growth are adaptations to the frequent fires that were common in the ponderosa's dry habitat. Another adaptation is rapid growth of a deep taproot. One-year-old, three-inch-tall ponderosas were found to have two-foot-long roots!

In the past, ponderosa pines formed open park-like stands. You can still get a sense of these magnificent forests in some parts of the Yosemite Valley.

With ponderosa are found the cinnamon-barked incense cedar, Douglas fir, white fir, sugar pine, Jeffrey pine, western white pine, and in places, the giant sequoia.

Douglas fir is typically a resident of moist coastal forests in California. It is uncommon in the Sierra, but can be found in the moister northern portion of the range. It is rare in the Sierra beyond Yosemite, and is not found south of the San Joaquin River. Like the ponderosa pine, the Douglas fir has a thick, corky bark to protect it from fires.

White fir was named for the white appearance of the grayish smooth bark of younger trees and the white underside of its flat, two- to three-inch-long needles. This is the typical "Christmas tree" of the Sierra, with branches reaching all the way to the ground. You'll seldom find a white fir cone because the cones of the true firs disintegrate on the branch. Shade tolerant, the white fir grows in the understory of ponderosa pine, sugar pine, and sequoia forests.

Sugar pine, one of the most magnificent of the Sierran pines, often grows to heights of 200 feet or more, with a beautiful straight bole.

Unfortunately, its size and straight grain made it attractive to lumbermen. As a result, old growth forests of this pine are rare outside protected areas like Yosemite National Park. The large cones, up to a foot or more in length, grow like pendant Christmas ornaments on outstretched branches.

Hardwoods include black oak, bigleaf maple, white alder, black cottonwood, aspen, mountain dogwood, and California hazelnut. Most of these species are restricted to riparian areas or moist sites.

The most common hardwood, the black oak, is scattered throughout the ponderosa pine zone. Due to its ability to sprout after a fire, the black oak dominates many sites where fires were frequent in the days prior to fire suppression. The dark, nearly black bark gives the tree its name. Its deciduous, six- to ten-inch, lobed, sharp-tipped leaves make it easy to identify. Many Sierran animals, from the black bear to the acorn woodpecker, depend upon the black oak acorns for their sustenance. Black oak acorns were the staple food for most west-slope Sierran Indian groups.

Big leaf maple has large leaves (up to 12 inches across) that turn a lovely yellow in the fall, lighting up the forest with a golden glow. These maples are common farther north in the moist coastal forests. Big leaf maple reaches its southern range limits in the Sierra, restricted primarily to moist canyons as far south as Kings Canyon–Sequoia National Park.

This mixed conifer forest belt is the premier fire zone of the Sierra. Fire was a frequent influence on the forest stand composition; thus it is not surprising that this zone has many species adapted to fire. As a rule, the pines, sequoia, incense cedar, and Douglas fir are all adapted to withstand periodic fire. Black oak survived by sprouting. White fir was one of the few species not tolerant of fire. Its numbers have increased dramatically as a consequence of fire suppression activities.

One can find chaparral species like deer brush, small-leafed ceanothus, greenleaf manzanita, and pinemat manzanita in the understory and small meadows of this forest zone. Other shrubs and flowers include bracken fern, bedstraw, mountain misery, thimbleberry, pinedrops, snow plant, false Solomon's seal, heartleaf arnica, California Indian pink, fireweed, leopard lily, wild rose, snowberry, and mountain pennyroyal.

Clockwise from above:
Redbud in bloom, Sequoia
National Park.
Rabbitbrush near Mt. Morrison.
Black oak below Cathedral Spires
in Yosemite National Park.
Red fir forest in winter at
Yosemite National Park.

Above: Dogwood in autumn at Tenaya Creek, Yosemite National Park.
Top left: Aspen along Lee Vining Creek, Inyo National Forest.
Left center: Joshua tree by Walker Pass in the southern Sierra.
Left: Foxtail pine in the Golden Trout Wilderness, Inyo National Forest.

51

Red Fir–Lodgepole Pine Zone

As you climb higher in the Sierra, snow deepens and you enter the "snow forest," or red fir–lodgepole pine zone. The greatest snowfall occurs here, with average annual precipitation up to 80 inches a year. Most of this falls as snow, which reaches average depths of 10 to 15 feet. The red fir–lodgepole pine forest ranges from 5,500 feet elevation in the north to as high as 10,000 feet elevation in the south, where it can properly be termed the lower subalpine forest. These woodlands, particularly those composed of lodgepole pine, are interspersed with meadows and much bare rock.

Red fir is so named because of the deep chocolate-rust color of its bark. This noble tree deserves its Latin name, *Abies magnifica*, that is, magnificent fir. Red fir is extremely common in the northern Sierra. Farther south, its distribution becomes spotty; the southernmost groves are found in northern Kern County.

Red fir generally occupies the deep, moist, well-drained soils of basins. Lodgepole dominates the rockier, less desirable sites. Other associated species on thin, rocky soils include western white pine, Jeffrey pine and western juniper. Red fir creates very open, even-aged stands. Its dense shade and litter accumulations keep other plants from getting established.

Lodgepole grows at higher elevations than the red fir. Although abundant bare rock limits the spread of fires in much of the subalpine zone of the Sierra, the lodgepole pines found here are well-adapted to regeneration after a blaze. Some lodgepole cones are serotinous, that is, they require heat for the scales to open and release seeds. In addition, this two-needled pine grows rapidly and can produce viable cones in as little as ten years. Once established on a recently burned area, it quickly fills in the forest with more of its kind. The widespread occurrence of even-aged stands of pine frequently indicates a previous fire.

Lodgepole pine, which also persists in the *absence* of fire, is successfully invading subalpine meadows. Past grazing practices disturbed natural sods and permitted tree invasion. Studies in Yosemite have documented that most meadow invasions began between 1890 and 1925, and later in other parts of the range.

Upper Subalpine Forest Zone

The upper subalpine forests of the Sierra are between 8,000 feet elevation in the north and to the limits of tree growth at 11,500 feet or more in the south. Open groves and scattered trees typify the subalpine zone, with great expanses of bare rock and meadows in between. Common trees of this zone include lodgepole pine, whitebark pine, mountain hemlock and foxtail pine.

Whitebark pine is the dominant subalpine species in much of the Sierra. It is rarer north of Lake Tahoe, and south of Whitney, but widely distributed in between. Whitebark pine, with its open-branched conformation, or its krummholz (stunted, sprawling) form at uppermost growing limits, is commonly seen on rocky ridges.

In spite of the hostile growing conditions, even small shrub-like trees may attain great age. John Muir counted the growth rings of a shrubby timberline specimen with a six-inch diameter trunk; that specimen was more than 400 years old. The nutritious seeds of the whitebark pine provide an important food source for many animals, including the chickaree squirrel and the vociferous Clark's nutcracker. Nutcrackers harvest seeds and cache them for winter and spring use, thereby helping to transport and plant the tree's seeds. In days gone by, the whitebark pine of the Sierra probably also supported grizzly bears, since the cone is a favorite and important food for grizzlies still surviving in the Rockies.

Foxtail pine is a distinctive timberline tree of the southern Sierra. It often forms pure stands of stately, stout trees with bright reddish bark, and boughs that look like a bottlebrush. It is common in the high country of Kings Canyon and Sequoia national parks and in the adjacent John Muir Wilderness. Foxtail is endemic to California, but the only other occurrence is in northern California's Klamath Mountains.

Foxtail pine never assumes a low, stunted krummholz form, remaining erect right up to the limits of growth. Like the related bristlecone pine, foxtail pine can continue to grow even with only a strip of live bark connecting its roots and branches. Due to the slow growth in its harsh environment, it often lives a thousand years or more.

While foxtail pine dominates the southern Sierra, mountain hemlock is characteristic of the northern parts of the range. Typically found in well-watered sites, largely from Yosemite north to Sierra Buttes, the mountain hemlock has a characteristic drooping crown that helps identify it even at a distance.

Western white pine is abundant on some rocky ridges. It is similar to the sugar pine, but smaller. These five-needled pines with reddish bark grow in open woodlands scattered on granite ridges from Yosemite north to Sierra Buttes. They are less common farther south, but are distributed all the way to southern Kern County.

Also found scattered on dry, rocky faces and windswept ridges are the long-lived, gnarly, weathered half-dead snags of western juniper that John Muir said seemed to live centuries on "sunshine and snow." Western junipers are estimated to survive for 3,000 years. In the Desolation Wilderness west of Lake Tahoe, you'll occasionally see this picturesque, stunted, wind-sheared ground-hugging tree.

Mountain Meadow Zone

Meadows are less common in the Sierra than in other mountain areas like the Rockies. Forests are more extensive, with fewer breaks. The meadows tend to follow stream corridors or low-lying basins where ground water remains close to the surface. Unlike the grasslands of the foothills, meadow plants rely upon summer moisture from seasonal snowpack for their survival. Thus, they are most common in the subalpine zone. Furthermore, meadows often indicate the last stages in lake succession; a pothole or lake basin has filled with sediments, but is still too wet to support trees.

Most Sierran meadows are composed mostly of sedges, not grasses. Tuolumne Meadow in Yosemite National Park is a prime example. Common meadow sedges include shorthair sedge, black sedge, Brewer's sedge, alpine sedge and beaked sedge. Sedges are closely related to grasses, and look like grasses, but have triangular stems and leaves in groups of threes. With the sedges grow true grasses, like tufted hairgrass, shorthair grass, and spiked trisetum.

Dozens of wildflowers, such as marsh marigold, shooting star, monkeyflower, geranium, paintbrush, elephant's head, camas, iris, and false hellebore also grow in the meadows. Various willow species and shrubby cinquefoil are common along streams and other wetlands. Most subalpine meadows have islands of trees, a feature that distinguishes them from true alpine areas.

Alpine Zone

Mountain meadows often advance above timberline. At the highest elevations, however, the true alpine zone has a distinctive flora of its own. Here no trees remain. Even the sturdiest and most enduring tree species require at least two months with average temperatures higher than 50 degrees Fahrenheit. Over much of the Sierra, such "balmy" conditions do not exist.

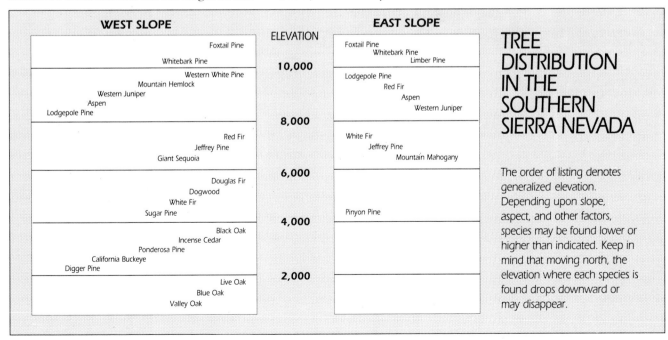

WEST SLOPE

Foxtail Pine		
Whitebark Pine		
Western White Pine		
Mountain Hemlock		
Western Juniper		
Aspen		
Lodgepole Pine		
Red Fir		
Jeffrey Pine		
Giant Sequoia		
Douglas Fir		
Dogwood		
White Fir		
Sugar Pine		
Black Oak		
Incense Cedar		
Ponderosa Pine		
California Buckeye		
Digger Pine		
Live Oak		
Blue Oak		
Valley Oak		

ELEVATION
10,000
8,000
6,000
4,000
2,000

EAST SLOPE

Foxtail Pine
Whitebark Pine
Limber Pine
Lodgepole Pine
Red Fir
Aspen
Western Juniper
White Fir
Jeffrey Pine
Mountain Mahogany
Pinyon Pine

TREE DISTRIBUTION IN THE SOUTHERN SIERRA NEVADA

The order of listing denotes generalized elevation. Depending upon slope, aspect, and other factors, species may be found lower or higher than indicated. Keep in mind that moving north, the elevation where each species is found drops downward or may disappear.

White fir grows in the understory of sequoias at Mariposa Grove, Yosemite National Park.

SEQUOIAS

"Walk the sequoia woods at any time of the year and you will say they are the most beautiful and majestic on earth."

–John Muir

If one were to pick out the quintessential Sierran tree, the vote would likely go to the giant sequoia. Related to the coast redwood, the giant sequoia lives nowhere in the world except along a 250-mile strip on the western slope of the Sierra Nevada. Even within its broad range, which runs from a grove of six trees in Placer County to the Deer Creek grove south of Sequoia National Park, the sequoia has a spotty distribution. Most trees are found in 75 isolated groves. The largest grove is on Redwood Mountain in Sequoia National Park. In total, sequoias cover approximately 35,000 acres.

The sequoia is arguably the largest living thing in the world. The tree may exceed 300 feet in height at about 800 years old. But it might live 3,000 years, continuing to add girth until death, attaining huge proportions. For instance, the Boole Tree on the Sequoia National Forest is 35.7 feet in diameter; Yosemite's Grizzly Giant is more than 30 feet in diameter. In some cases, individual branches on these immense trees are larger than entire trees elsewhere—the largest limb on the General Sherman Tree is 150 feet long and more than 6.8 feet in diameter!

The sequoia's spotty distribution has puzzled people for decades. Why are the trees only found on the west slope of the Sierra, and why only in groves? No single answer has unanimous support. Research, however, has shown that the trees do have some exacting requirements for their survival.

Nearly all sequoia groves grow in areas of deep soil where summer moisture levels remain high. The seedlings require bare mineral soil and full sunlight. For this reason, fires are important to the survival and continued existence of the sequoia. Fires not only remove many of the overstory trees, permitting light to penetrate to the forest floor, but fire also exposes the bare mineral soil necessary for seedling establishment. Periodic fire also removes competing understory species that would otherwise use up water and mineral supplies.

As a species adapted to fire, the sequoia has few peers. Its reddish bark—often up to two feet thick—protects the inner living tissue from all but the hottest fires. Another example of the sequoia's fire adaptation is its ability to self-prune. Older trees lose their lower limbs, thus removing a potential "ladder" for flames to reach the fire-sensitive crown.

Sequoia cones open only after they have dried out. The heat from fires assures that cone scales will open, providing an abundant source of seeds. It was the dependency of sequoia on fires that led to some of the nation's first prescribed burn programs. An active fire and fuel reduction program exists within both Yosemite and Sequoia national parks.

Two creatures also help disperse sequoia seeds. The long-horned beetle tunnels into sequoia cones, eating a few seeds, and destroying the cones' vascular connections to the tree. As a consequence, the cones dry out and the seeds are released. The Douglas squirrel is a little more noticeable than the beetle. This gray, energetic, rodent eats the scales of sequoia cones and often spits out the seeds, dispersing them widely over the forest floor. Further, 140 insects depend upon the sequoia in one way or another.

The first whites to observe the sequoia were members of Joseph Walker's trapping party who crossed the Sierra in 1883 to what is now Yosemite National Park. The expedition journals were lost until the turn of the century, so credit for discovery often goes to A.T. Dowd, a hunter, who in 1852 stumbled upon the Calaveras Grove of Big Trees while chasing a wounded bear. News of the giant trees quickly spread through the mining camps along the foothills of the Sierra. The discovery of (and later the desire to protect) the Mariposa sequoia grove in what is now Yosemite National Park was one of the reasons for the creation of the new park. Given the relative rarity and magnificence of the sequoia, it is not surprising that Sequoia National Park was established in large measure to protect the best specimens found in the Sierra.

The future of the sequoia, however, remains in some doubt. Global warming may jeopardize their continued existence if climate change is too rapid for adjustments. The greatest immediate threat is posed by the continued policy of fire suppression, particularly outside of the national parks. Suppression continues to permit excessive fuel levels to build up throughout the Sierra. One day, catastrophic fires may wipe out even the larger, older sequoia trees.

Visitors to Sequoia National Park viewing a cross-section of a sequoia. Sequoias may live more than 3,000 years.

Here only low-growing shrubs and flowering plants survive, often requiring five to ten years of very modest growth during the short growing season to store sufficient energy to produce a flower blossom.

Compared to other alpine zones in the United States and Canada, the Sierra Nevada alpine is among the warmest and sunniest. A significant number of desert species have migrated upslope. Most alpine floras rarely exceed one percent annual species, but about six percent of Sierran alpine plants are annuals. This is likely an adaptation to the arid conditions and unreliable moisture of the High Sierra.

The Sierra Nevada has fewer circumpolar arctic species than other alpine zones—only 10 percent have arctic affiliation. Instead, the unusual number of endemic specimens indicates the zone's isolation from the main body of arctic flora farther to the north. In total, approximately 600 plants inhabit the Sierra Nevada alpine zone, although about 400 of these are found at lower elevations as well.

As with other major plant communities, the alpine zone is at lower elevations in the north and at higher elevations in the south. Typically, alpine plants are found above 9,500 feet in the Lake Tahoe area, and over 11,000 feet by the time you reach the Kings Canyon–Sequoia area in the south. Although most alpine species do not grow above the 13,000-foot level, I've encountered a few well-protected plants growing above 14,000 feet on Mt. Whitney.

North of Tahoe the alpine zone is largely absent. South of the high peaks in the Whitney region, only Olancha Peak harbors alpine plant communities. Between these two areas, however, the alpine zone is large, encompassing most of the higher basins, ridges, and peaks, particularly in the upper Kings and Kern river drainages.

Alpine plants have several distinctive adaptations to their environment. They must survive rapid, large, diurnal temperature changes; a short growing season; and harsh, cold winds. As a result, the alpine plants tend to be dwarfed. The short growing season and high winds make tall stems and large leaves impractical, as well as unnecessary. Most alpine plants assume a low, compact, mat-like, cushion or rosette habit. Alpine species, however, sport showy blossoms of normal size that attract pollinators such as mosquitoes, bumblebees, flies and butterflies.

Many alpine plants have hairs on their stems and leaves. This helps the plant trap radiant solar energy and retain heat. The hairs also reduce evaporative losses. Other species accomplish the same thing with leathery, waxy leaves.

Another common characteristic of alpine plants is vegetative reproduction. Growing from bulbs, rhizomes or stems permits plants to survive even where sexual reproduction via flowers and seeds seldom occurs.

Alpine plant communities are defined according to the substrate on which they grow. The most common divisions are meadows, rock gardens, and boulder fields, all with their own characteristic plants. Common alpine flowers include alpine shooting star, greater elephant's head, alpine buttercup, alpine everlasting, white mountain heather, alpine laurel, Sierra primrose, mountain sorrel, dwarf Lewisia, spreading phlox, alpine lupine, Lemmon's draba, sky pilot, cutleaf daisy, and red mountain heather.

East-side Flora

Due to rainshadow effects, the east side of the Sierra Nevada is considerably drier than the west slope and is influenced by the close proximity of the Great Basin Desert. Bishop, in the Owens Valley along the eastern foot of the Sierra escarpment, lies at 4,140 feet and receives six inches of precipitation a year. Comparable sites on the western slope get 25 to 30 inches. Although many of the same species encountered on the west slope can be found on the east slope, in this drier environment they are more localized. Also, due to greater precipitation with increasing elevation, the east-slope plants are typically found at higher elevations than their west slope counterparts.

For instance, one can find black oak (a common west-slope deciduous tree) growing along Onion Creek near Independence. Red fir, another typically west-slope tree, is fairly common near Mammoth Mountain. Neither, however, is abundant on the east slope. White fir is well distributed, but only in the wetter areas. Ponderosa pine is common on the east slope north of Mono Lake, but absent south of there, where Jeffrey pine, its close relative, dominates. In fact, the largest pure Jeffrey pine forest in the world sprawls out across the volcanic craters and highlands near Mammoth Lakes. Washoe pine, closely related to Jeffrey pine, is found only in the Carson Range near Lake Tahoe.

Conversely, some species found here and there on the western slope become common east of the crest. The beautiful, white-barked, trembling aspen forms extensive parklands and groves along east-side streams and among higher basins, particularly in the Conway Summit area. Yet it tends to be found only in scattered, small groves on the west slope.

Aspen tend to grow as clones. You can observe the genetically related groups on a hillside in autumn. You will note some aspen with green leaves, while immediately adjacent will be others with leaves in full autumn golden glory, while yet another group may have dropped its leaves altogether. Each of these groups defines a different clone.

Aspen generally develop from suckers, not seeds. Thus, they repeatedly reoccupy sites that are burned, repeatedly swept by avalanches, or otherwise disturbed. Some have suggested that aspen in the Sierra may have persisted by suckering since the last glacial period, potentially making them one of the "oldest" living trees.

Curl-leaf mountain mahogany, an evergreen shrub-tree, is more abundant on the drier eastern side. Water birch, known from the upper Kerns–Kings rivers, is almost totally restricted to east-side riparian corridors. Some species, like limber pine, are only found along the eastern slope, often replacing or intermixing with whitebark pine in the higher-elevation subalpine forests.

One of the most characteristic trees of the east slope is single leaf pinyon pine, a short squat tree seldom growing over 30 feet tall, which produces a round cone with large edible nuts. Pinyon nuts were a steady source of food for east-side Indian people as well as for many native wildlife species. Pinyon is common on the southern and eastern side of the Kern Plateau in the South Sierra and Domeland wildernesses, and only rarely occurs on the western slope.

At the lowest elevations, one encounters a vast sea of gray sagebrush, one of the dominant shrubs of the Great Basin Desert. There are a number of different sagebrush species and subspecies found along the east slope. The most common is *Artemisia tridentata*, or Great Basin big sage. Also found are low sage, spiny sagebrush, and silver sage. Other important shrubs in the sagebrush zone include curl-leaf mountain mahogany, rubber rabbitbrush, and antelope bitterbrush.

Domestic livestock do not typically eat sagebrush, and sagebrush has increased in number and distribution because of decades of overgrazing. Overgrazing hinders wildfires. With grass removed as a fuel, fire-intolerant sagebrush easily spreads. Soil erosion resulting from overgrazing has stripped away topsoil and increased gully formation. Recovery is unlikely.

Livestock have devastated many of the Great Basin grassland–sagebrush ecosystems. These plant communities evolved in the absence of large hoofed ungulates. There were no bison here, nor even large herds of elk. Antelope and localized populations of bighorn sheep were the largest herbivores found on the east side of the Sierra. As a consequence, the composition of the native ecosystems changed due to the impact of countless hooves and mouths of domestic livestock. Studies have shown that, under pristine conditions, sagebrush typically made up 10 to 15 percent of the ground cover, while perennial grasses such as bluebunch wheatgrass, Idaho fescue, needle and thread grass, and basin wild rye dominated the landscape. Today, finding these grasses at all is at times difficult.

At the very southern end of the eastern Sierra grow species common in the high desert portions of the Mojave Desert, like the white-blossomed Joshua tree and desert sage (a true sage or salvia).

FIRE ECOLOGY

"The inviting openness of the Sierra woods is one of their most distinguishing characteristics. The trees of all the species stand more or less apart in groves, or in small irregular groups, enabling one to find a way nearly everywhere, along sunny colonnades and through openings that have a smooth, park-like surface, strewn with brown needles and burrs...One would experience but little difficulty in riding a horse through the successive belts all the way up to the storm-beaten fringes of the icy peaks." So wrote John Muir in the 1880s.

Right: Jeffrey pine cones at Donner State Park. Most Sierra Nevada pines are fire tolerant.

Facing page: Fire scar on a giant sequoia in Grant Grove, Kings Canyon National Park. Sequoias have bark up to two feet thick to protect them from the frequent fires that burn through Sierran forests.

Although some Sierran forests are still uncluttered and without a trail, most people would find it toilsome to ride a horse, or even walk, through many of the mid-elevation west-slope forests of today. The congested and dense forest growth is the result of 100 years of fire suppression. This has serious consequences for both forest ecosystems and the humans who live and recreate in the Sierra.

While researching this book, I stopped by the Tahoe Basin National Forest office to discuss the fire policies on the forest. I said to the fire control officer that the large number of dead and dying trees in the Tahoe Basin could be a recipe for disaster in the basin. He corrected me by replying "We have a disaster waiting to happen from Mexico to Canada!"

Some might say the disaster has already occurred. According to a recent Forest Service report, the large amount of dead and dying forest in the Sierra is a result of several factors.

The first is that logging was too often targeted at the best trees for timber cutting. Hence the forest suffers from a loss in genetic diversity, which reduces the ability of trees to resist disease, insects or drought.

In addition, livestock grazing has too frequently removed the fine fuels (mostly grass) that in the past supported low-intensity fires. Livestock grazing has resulted in compacted soils and has induced watershed changes, thus increasing the vulnerability of forests to drought.

The report, however, singled out fire suppression policies as the single biggest factor in the creation of the present forest ecosystem calamity. Wildfires in the Sierra Nevada forests are a certainty. It is not a matter of "if," but "when."

The present increase of dead trees is in part nature's way of correcting past imbalances. Historical observations from around the country show that outbreaks of insects and diseases have occurred in the past and are a natural part of the forest ecosystem. While it may appear that trees are dying from insects or disease, ultimately the cause is related to the dense thickets created by fire exclusion. The thickets exacerbate the effects of insect, disease or drought.

Accounts by Muir and others, combined with old photos, make it clear that most of the Sierran forests were park-like as a result of periodic cleansing by fire. Some of these fires were lightning-caused. In other cases, fires were set by Indians. In either case, there were many fires that remained low intensity, primarily killing saplings, reducing fuel accumulations and litter, but seldom destroying the larger, mature trees.

Fire frequency varied with elevation. The history of an area's past fires is recorded in scars on older trees. These fire scar histories show that fires typically burned through the forests every 3 to 10 years in lower elevation savanna–grasslands. The interval between fires increased at higher elevations, where conditions were wetter and the fire season shorter due to lingering snowpacks. Here, fires tended to be larger and of greater intensity, due to higher fuel loadings. This generalization does not apply to the subalpine forests near timberline, where a lack of fuels, coupled with vast expanses of rock, meant fires were again of low-intensity and spread slowly, if at all.

Nevertheless, although the majority of fires remained small, the occasional large fire accounted for most of the acreage burned. Such high intensity fires were infrequent, but might burn hundreds of thousands, even millions, of acres at one time. Typically, such large fires started as a number of individual small fires. Under the right conditions, they expanded, eventually joining into a massive fire complex with a front that might extend over dozens of miles.

As a result of fire suppression efforts, vegetative communities changed. Shade-tolerant species like white fir increased; accumulations of dead and downed wood increased (referred to as fuel loading); and shade-intolerant species like sequoia and some pines declined or were crowded out by the fir. In addition, species that sprout after fire, like black oak, declined as well. For example, early photos of the Yosemite Valley show far more oak groves than exist today—partly a result of fire suppression in the valley. Trees have also invaded subalpine meadows and other forest openings, reducing the overall acreage of this important wildlife habitat type.

While there is much evidence to suggest that wildfire plays a critical ecological role in the Sierra Nevada forest ecosystems, we have a decidedly negative view of it. Repeatedly we hear how such and such a fire "destroyed" so many acres of forest, or that the forest is "recovering" from the fire, just as a person might recover from a disease or illness. Yet fire is not a disease or illness. Fire is to a forest what exercise is to human health. As periodic exercise contributes to human fitness, periodic fires contribute to the forest ecosystem's fitness in many parts of the West.

One of the most important ecological functions of fire is nutrient cycling. Unlike eastern deciduous forests, where moist, warm summers favor decomposition by bacteria, fungi and other biological agents, the Sierran forests are dominated by pronounced summer drought, and litter and downed logs decompose slowly, if at all. Without decomposition, nutrients removed from the soil by plant growth remain bound up in the dead litter that accumulates on the ground and as standing dead snags. It is fire, not biological agents, that releases these bound nutrients and returns them to the soils for new forest growth.

Fires do more than recycle nutrients. Fires remove duff from the forest floor and expose bare mineral soil, a requirement for the germination of some tree seedlings. By killing saplings and even mature trees, fires reduce competition and thin the forest—much as a wolf might thin a deer herd—thereby ensuring more water, nutrients and sunlight for the trees that survive the blaze.

Furthermore, fires often cleanse a forest of pathogens. Heat kills fungi and tree diseases in the soil. It kills many predatory insects that live in downed logs or in the upper layers of the soil. Even the smoke from fires has been shown to kill forest pathogens.

Fires may even contribute to soil production. The rapid heating and subsequent cooling associated with blazes frequently cracks rocks and boulders, reducing them to smaller pieces, thus speeding soil formation. Repeated over and over for thousands of years, such a process may actually be essential to soil development.

Fuel build-up has been most significant in the zone between 4,000 and 9,000 feet elevation, where moisture, soils and climatic conditions are most conducive to rapid forest growth. As a consequence of fire suppression, the intervals between fires have lengthened, and blazes tend be more intense, hotter, and burn more acreage. Above 9,000 feet, plant growth is limited by temperature and a short growing season. Even with a hundred years of fire suppression, fuel loadings have not increased significantly at higher elevations.

In some parts of the Sierra, primarily in wilderness areas and national parks, most naturally ignited fires are permitted to burn unrestricted under certain predetermined prescriptions. For instance, in 1968, 75 percent of Kings Canyon–Sequoia national parks was designated a natural fire management zone where fire suppression would not occur except under the most unusual circumstances.

Driving cattle out of park at Bond Pass, 1941.

61

Clockwise from above: Ponderosa pine bark sloughs off when heated, which helps to protect the tree from flames.

Backpacker walks through charred forest in Yosemite National park. The snags provide excellent habitat for woodpeckers and other cavity nesters.

Western juniper snags near Susie Lake, Desolation Wilderness, Tahoe Basin National Forest. Fires were relatively infrequent at higher subalpine forests of the Sierra.

Left: Domestic livestock are responsible for degradation of more miles of riparian habitat than any human factor. This has serious consequences for everything from trout to birds, which depend upon streamside vegetation for nesting and feeding habitat. Soil compaction also speeds runoff, exacerbating the effects of drought. Domeland Wilderness.

Below: Digger pine and chaparral near Dobbins in the Sierra Nevada foothills. Chaparral plants are dependent on fires to remove competing vegetation. They can sprout from their roots after a fire, and even have volatile oils in their leaves that ensure they will burn.

Since fire was a natural and frequent ecological force in the Sierra Nevada forests, it is not surprising that much of the flora has adaptations that permit the plants to survive, and sometimes thrive, under a fire regime. The giant sequoia is a good example of a fire-adapted species. Its thick bark protects the growing cambium layer from all but the hottest blazes. Mature trees also self-prune, losing their lower branches as they grow, thereby reducing the opportunities for a surface fire to jump into the tree canopy. Finally, sequoia cones are serotinous, which means the scales that contain the seeds remain closed until heated. Thus, after a fire has burned through a sequoia grove and removed the duff and litter that prevents seedling germination, a shower of seeds is released from the recently heated cones.

Other Sierran tree species exhibiting some of these same traits include the ponderosa pine and Jeffrey pine, both of which self-prune and have thick bark, protection for the mature tree. Though lodgepole pine has thin bark, it, like sequoia, produces serotinous cones.

Another adaptation to fire is root sprouting. Many chaparral brush species like manzanita and ceanothus sprout from their roots. Thus, if the above-ground stems are burned, the shrubs quickly sprout new stems from the underground root crown. Sprouting after fires is not restricted to just shrubs. Both aspen and black oak sprout from their roots after fire.

Species like white fir are not adapted to fires. They display none of the above features. White fir bark is thin, offering little protection from flames or heat. Branches reach nearly to the ground, which allows fires to "ladder" up into the canopy. Finally, the white fir cone is non-serotinous, that is, no extra seed is held in preparation for fire.

While fire suppression may be effective under normal conditions, in times of drought, particularly if blazes are driven by winds, no amount of suppression seems to halt them—no matter how much money is spent or how many fire fighters are assigned to combat the inferno. Invariably, when burning conditions change—either the fire burns into the alpine, rocky terrain and runs out of fuel, or the weather changes to snow or rain—fire fighters finally gain "control" of a blaze.

In recent years, more and more people have built their dream cabins in the woods. Fire suppression agencies are obligated to fight any fire, no matter how fruitless the effort. Building in forested areas is no different from building on the flood plains of rivers. Though the river may not flood every year, high water eventually will inundate the dwellings. The same is true of fire occurrence in most of the Sierra Nevada.

Much stricter attention should be placed on just where people are permitted to build homes or other structures. This could be accomplished by zoning, just as we zone river flood plains. Also, houses could be grouped together so they are easier to defend when the inevitable blaze does occur.

Since we can't really prevent fires, we need to follow the lead of the Sierran forests and adapt to blazes. It is far less expensive to make targets defensible than to suppress, or attempt to suppress, all fires. Instead of funneling money into fighting fires, we should invest in making safe, defensible places where we don't invite catastrophic fires. This can be accomplished by fuel removal, via either prescribed burn or selective and limited timber harvest.

Finally, taxpayers in general bear the cost of fire suppression, not the homeowners themselves. Higher taxes on dwellings in high-risk zones, or far from fire-fighting stations, would ensure that those receiving service assume more of the fire suppression cost.

Above: South Fork Yuba River, Mother Lode country.
Left: Pack string crossing Mono Pass in the John Muir Wilderness, Inyo National Forest.

Top: Bear Creek Spire reflected in small tarn in the John Muir Wilderness, Inyo National Forest.
Right: North from Sonora Peak in the Carson–Iceberg Wilderness.

Facing page: El Capitan and Merced River, Yosemite National Park. El Capitan is one of the largest granite faces in the world.

Above: Beach at Sugar Pine State Park, Lake Tahoe. Lake Tahoe is the tenth-deepest lake in the world.
Left: Tarn from Glen Pass on John Muir Trail in Kings Canyon National Park.

Facing page: Evening glow along John Muir Trail near Mt. Whitney in Sequoia National Park.

Above: Tule River by Coffee Camp in the Sequoia National Forest.
Right: Lone Pine Peak at dawn from Alabama Hills.

Facing page: Lichen-encrusted granite along Tuolumne River in Tuolumne Meadows looking toward Lembert Dome, Yosemite National Park.

Left: Early wooden trail leading to Vernal Falls in Yosemite National Park.
Below: Using oxen to haul logs from the woods.

Facing page: East Fork of the Carson River in Toiyabe National Forest.

WILDLIFE

The Sierra Nevada still has most of its native wildlife species, at least in small relict populations. That does not mean that the Sierra Nevada has not suffered. Gone today are the grizzly bear and the California condor. Many other species are rare, and exist at much lower numbers than in the past. These includes species like the Sierran red fox, wolverine, fisher, bighorn sheep, harlequin duck, Little Kern River golden trout, great gray owl, and the well-publicized spotted owl. As more and more habitat is subdivided, logged, flooded by dams, or overgrazed to dust, the Sierra's list of wildlife species extinct or extirpated will only grow. Each of these animals acts as a proverbial "canary in the coal mine" and in the Sierra the canary is dying.

Right: Red-tailed hawk.

Facing page: The only bears left in the Sierra are black bears, which have several color phases, including brown. Grizzly bears are now extinct in the Sierra.

CONRAD ROWE

A few species and animal groups are now more common. For example, in Yosemite National Park trout were unknown above 4,000 feet in elevation. All fish currently found in subalpine and alpine waters were stocked, and many previously barren waters throughout the Sierran high country now have fish populations.

A recent Forest Service publication counts 26 amphibian, 27 reptile, 208 bird, and 94 mammal species in the Sierra. Some 57 more bird species are occasionally seen, but are considered accidental or unusual.

There are thousands of invertebrates, from insects to snails, many barely known to science. We learn year by year that these animals are perhaps more important to the overall ecological health of the earth than the larger animals typically discussed in texts like this. I, unfortunately, have the same bias and lack of knowledge regarding these lesser-known species as most other people. Though this chapter will focus on the major vertebrate species and groups, be aware that this does not imply that these species are of greater value.

Fish

Fish were not found in many high-elevation Sierran waters prior to the coming of the white man's stocking programs. On the west slope, with the exception of the Kern River, trout were not known to live above 4,000 feet. On the east side, there were no trout in the Owens River or tributaries. While most high-country lakes lacked fish, there were exceptions. Lake Tahoe, for example, had immense native cutthroat trout. Many west-slope streams had spawning runs of chinook salmon and native trout along their lower reaches. The salmon are now largely gone due to dams.

Three trout species are native to the Sierra—rainbow, golden and cutthroat. On the west slope, rainbow trout were found in most major rivers draining into the San Joaquin and the Sacramento.

Cutthroat trout were native to the major drainages in the Lahontan Basin, primarily the Walker, Truckee (which includes Lake Tahoe) and Carson rivers. The Paiute cutthroat, a rare subspecies, is only known from one Sierran location, Fish Creek, in the Carson–Iceberg Wilderness.

The golden trout is endemic to the Kern River; transplants have significantly increased distribution throughout the Sierra and the West.

It is thought that golden trout evolved from rainbow trout after a long period of isolation. Hybrids generally result where the two are stocked together.

There are two forms of golden trout—Volcano Creek and Little Kern. Competition with non-native brook trout and inbreeding with introduced rainbows threatened the genetic purity and survival of the Little Kern breed. By the 1970s there were fewer than five isolated genetically pure populations within tributaries of the Little Kern River. The golden trout was subsequently listed as an Endangered Species in 1977. The Forest Service and California Fish and Game have embarked on a program to eradicate the non-native rainbows and hybrids from the Little Kern drainage in the appropriately named Golden Trout Wilderness to make this a sanctuary for this fish.

Three additional kinds of trout now found in the Sierra are the result of transplants. They include eastern brook trout from the eastern United States, brown trout imported from Europe, and the lake trout brought from the Midwest. A transplant in Lake Tahoe is the Kokanee salmon, a landlocked version of the familiar Pacific sockeye salmon.

Native Sierran fish include the mountain whitefish, western sucker, Sacramento squawfish, Lahontan mountain sucker, speckled dace, Lahontan redsides, hardhead, Tui chub, and various sculpins.

Although popular with the public and with state Fish and Game agencies, fish stocking has had many unfortunate consequences. In some cases, native fish have become hybridized—a common occurrence with rainbow and cutthroat trout—eliminating some important genetic diversity. When fish are moved, there can be a loss of local genetic adaptations. For example, timing of spawning in any particular body of water is often genetically based and may be fine-tuned to local conditions. In addition, native fish like cutthroat trout sometimes have been displaced by exotic fish like brook trout or brown trout.

Besides the impact on fish, stocking waters where no fish previously existed can upset or destroy non-piscine aquatic ecosystems. Research in the North Cascades has demonstrated that introduction of fish has substantially changed the invertebrate fauna of mountain lakes, even causing extinction of some species. Fish stocking may be responsible for a major decline in some Sierra Nevada amphibians.

Amphibians and Reptiles

Amphibians and reptiles are cold-blooded animals, absorbing warmth from their surroundings. Hence, they tend to be active only during the warmer months of the year. Except for species living at the lowest elevations, most hibernate during the winter. Some amphibians even manage to live in the cool, subalpine reaches at 11,000 feet or more.

Nine salamanders are known to occur in the Sierra. Most are secretive and not likely to be seen. Among the most widely distributed are the tiger, long-toed, California newt, ensatina, arboreal, and California slender salamanders. A few species have very restricted distribution, including the Mount Lyell and the limestone salamanders.

The more common toads and frogs are the Pacific tree frog, red-legged frog, western toad, foothills and mountain yellow-legged frogs, and the uncommon Yosemite toad.

Recent research shows an alarming decline in many amphibians throughout the West. The Sierra Nevada is no exception. Eight out of 22 species of amphibians known to occur in the Sierra Nevada may soon be extinct over most or all of their range. This includes such species as the California red-legged frog, foothills yellow-legged frog, mountain yellow-legged frog, Yosemite toad, and Mount. Lyell salamander and limestone salamander. The foothills yellow-legged frog is now considered extinct in Sequoia National Park, although as late as the 1960s it was common there.

The reasons for the decline appear to vary from species to species. In some cases, there is no clear-cut "smoking gun." Nevertheless, a few human influences may account for some, if not all, of the observed declines. In areas with heavy logging or livestock grazing, changes in watershed flows and damage to riparian areas can cause water tables to drop, or reduce the amphibian's hiding cover significantly, thus decreasing habitat quality and quantity. These impacts effectively fragment the habitat, as logging fragments old-growth forests for spotted owls. Small, isolated populations may die out due to random population fluctuations, but are less likely to be recolonized by nearby populations if no close sources exist because of fragmentation.

Declines also have been noted even in protected areas like Yosemite National Park, where neither grazing nor logging occurs. Here the losses appear to be related to fish-stocking programs. Trout eat frog eggs, tadpoles and adults, and consequently reduce or effectively eliminate these amphibians from many otherwise suitable waters. In Yosemite, for example, all 339 mountain lakes were once fishless. Today about one-third of them support fish populations—many of them maintained in the past by stocking programs. Although frogs obviously exist in other areas that do have fish, it may be that in the harsh subalpine environments amphibians cannot sustain large losses and maintain their numbers over time. Today, partially out of concern for the health of amphibians, neither Kings Canyon–Sequoia nor Yosemite permits stocking of high-country lakes. Many lakes may still retain fish because existing populations are self-perpetuating.

Unlike amphibians, reptiles are not confined to moist locations, and hence are more widely distributed in the Sierra.

Most lizards prey on insects. Among the common species of lizards are the sagebrush lizard, fence lizard, northern alligator lizard, and Gilbert's skink.

An especially interesting lizard is the California legless lizard, which through evolution has lost its legs and now resembles a snake. This is an adaptation to its burrowing habit—legs would be a hindrance instead of an asset. The legless lizard is found only in the Kaweah and lower Kern drainages.

Common snakes include the rubber boa, ringneck snake, sharp-tailed snake, racer and striped racer, common kingsnake, gopher snake, mountain king snake, common garter snake, western aquatic garter snake, and western rattlesnake.

If the legless lizard is an example of the intermediate step that lizards may have taken during the evolution into snakes, then the rubber boa shows this relationship in the opposite direction. Unlike most other snakes, it has vestal legs in the form of anal spurs.

Garter snakes bear their young alive (as do the western rattlers), which may be one reason they can survive at colder high elevations. The most likely snake to be encountered is the western terrestrial garter snake, common in the subalpine reaches of the Sierra.

Birds

Over 300 species of birds can be considered Sierra Nevada residents or migrants. At least two species once found in the Sierra are

Right: The pygmy owl is dependent upon cavities for nesting.
Below: Yellow-bellied marmot. Since marmots hibernate most of the year, they must gain enough fat during the brief summer to sustain them in their burrows.

Top: Bighorn sheep were once abundant along the entire eastern slope of the Sierra, but due to disease and competition from domestic sheep, bighorns are reduced to a few scattered populations.
Left: Coyotes are common at all elevations.

ALAN & SANDY CAREY

now extirpated—the California condor and Bell's vireo. Other species are in decline, generally due to human habitat manipulation and changes. The willow flycatcher, once common, is now reduced to 200 breeding pairs in the entire Sierra. This is primarily due to habitat losses resulting from dam construction and from livestock degradation of riparian habitat. The great gray owl has also suffered a similar fate. Its numbers have dropped to an estimated 50 birds, in part as a result of livestock grazing of meadows that brought about a reduction in its food supply of voles and mice.

The northern spotted owl is the center of controversy. The owl is in decline, primarily due to excessive timber harvest of the old-growth forest habitat it requires. The owl uses old-growth trees in several ways. The primary species upon which it preys are flying squirrels, voles, and other small rodents found in the multilayered canopy, old snags, and fallen logs that characterize "ancient forests." The northern spotted owl also nests in cavities that are abundant only in older forests with many snags and rotted trees. In addition, the multi-layered canopy of older trees is essential to the owl's thermal regulation, providing the cool shade needed in summer and protection from snow and rain in winter.

Finally, predation upon young spotted owls by other birds—including other owls—occurs with higher frequency outside of old-growth forest habitat. As logging fragments the forest, young birds attempting to colonize adjacent, but fragmented, habitat are more vulnerable to predation.

Another bird associated with the mature, old-growth forests is the pileated woodpecker. Nearly as large as a crow with a "Woody Woodpecker" red crest contrasting with a black and white body, the pileated lives among the large trees of the mid-elevations. The pileated woodpecker is seldom seen, but often heard. Its loud drumming as it chisels insects from old, dead snags often resonates through the forest. Other tell-tale signs are the large rectangular holes the bird carves into snags when searching for grubs and insects. The cavities it carves provide suitable homes for other cavity-nesting species like the wood duck and spotted owl. As logging clearcuts fragment more and more of the forest, substituting young trees for "decadent old snags," the pileated and many other species dependent upon ancient forests will surely decline in number.

The acorn woodpecker is another cavity nester. These brightly-colored birds live in colonies located in oak forests. They form cooperative breeding groups somewhat like wolves; some adults breed, others act as helpers, and both obtain food and defend the nest. Acorn woodpeckers collect mast and store it in holes chipped in trees or fence posts—such granaries are a sure sign of the presence of the species.

The water dipper was one of John Muir's favorite birds. Living along fast-moving streams, this plump, gray wren-like bird dives underwater and walks on the bottom to hunt insects. It has a peculiar habit of bobbing up and down as it scans the water from rocky streamside perches.

Brown cowbirds are so called because of their close association with domestic livestock. The cowbird has greatly expanded its range due to the introduction of livestock and packstock into the Sierra, along with the logging and urbanization that has opened up formerly timbered habitat.

The expanded cowbird population has serious consequences for many other bird species because cowbirds are nest parasites. They lay their eggs in another bird's nest. The parasitized bird then raises the young cowbird as if it were its own, often to the detriment of its own young. Some suspect Bell's vireo has died out in the Sierra partly because of cowbird nest parasitism. The willow flycatcher, solitary vireo, warbling vireo, and yellow warblers have all declined due to cowbird parasitism. Thus, some assert, livestock grazing and packstock use of the Sierra contributes to the spread of cowbirds, and threatens the native biodiversity of this range.

Campers in Yosemite or elsewhere in the Sierra are likely to be familiar with the Steller's jay. These noisy, bold, blue birds seek handouts from humans. Typically associated with forest habitats, the Steller's jay is found throughout the mixed conifer zone.

Another jay often seen in the high country is the Clark's nutcracker. These black, gray and white birds nest throughout the whitebark pine zone. One jay may harvest up to 30,000 pine seeds a year, caching them for future use, and in the process, planting whitebark pines throughout the mountains. Most Sierran nutcrackers breed on the east slope, often in mid-winter while snow still covers the ground.

The tame, gray-crowned rosy finch is one of the most common birds of the wind-swept snowy alpine country. I even saw one foraging on top of Mt. Whitney! Many of them can winter in the alpine, subsisting on seeds found on windblown ridges and peaks.

While "tame" birds like the rosy finch and Steller's jay may be seen with some regularity, the blue grouse is more likely to be heard than seen. In the spring, the male blue grouse "hoots" with low deep notes that sound something like a person blowing across the top of a pop bottle. Because of its ventriloquist quality, it is difficult to locate a "hooting" grouse. It tends to be associated with thick red fir and pine forests, often near streams. Unlike many other birds, the blue grouse does not migrate to lower elevations in winter. Rather, it moves upslope into thick timber, where protection from winter storms is assured.

The rufous hummingbird is a tiny alpine bird that could be mistaken for a large bumblebee. The male rufous hummingbird is a ruddy red color, as the name implies; the female is green with a white breast and looks like many other female hummers.

The hummingbird has one of the highest metabolism rates of any bird, due to its small size and the energy demands of its whirring wings. To survive, it requires high-calorie food like flower nectar. It is not uncommon to see these tiny birds darting in and among the subalpine and alpine flower gardens of the Sierra searching for patches of "ripe" flowers.

Hummingbirds conserve energy by entering a torpor during the cold nights that characterize high elevations. Torpor is a kind of hibernation that reduces energy losses by slowing metabolism and permitting the body temperature to drop closer to the ambient air temperature.

Although common in the Sierra, rufous hummingbirds do not breed here. All the birds seen in summer are migrants from as far away as Alaska.

The mountain chickadee, a petite black and white bird only slightly larger than the hummingbird, experiences many of the same problems of maintaining body temperatures as the hummingbird. The chickadee is one of the few birds that remains year-round in the higher Sierran forests. Because the chickadee has such small volume to produce heat and large surface area to lose it, this bird must eat an enormous amount of high-energy food to survive. This typically means either insects or seeds, both of which are high in fat and carbohydrates.

Brewer's blackbirds are probably the most common birds seen around the picnic grounds in the Yosemite Valley. These black, glossy birds have piercing yellow eyes and a hint of metallic in their feathers. They can be seen strutting about the parking lots and campgrounds, wherever people abound. Although they breed in the foothills, they range up into the ponderosa pine–black oak zone, such as in Yosemite Valley. When not living off tourist handouts, the birds rely upon seeds and insects.

The dark-eyed junco, a seed and insect eater, is common along trails. These sparrow-like birds with white-edged tailfeathers and dark heads often form large flocks in late summer and dart from place to place, particularly in open meadows and along the edges of forest clearings.

Birds by Habitat Type

The following is a brief listing of birds commonly associated with specific habitat types and elevations. Keep in mind, however, that many birds can be found in more than one habitat depending upon the season of the year.

Grasslands, savanna, and chaparral (500 to 5,000 feet): western bluebird, northern harrier, kestrel, mourning dove, horned lark, western bluebird, turkey vulture, acorn woodpecker, red-tailed hawk, Brewer's blackbird, western kingbird, grasshopper sparrow, ash-throated flycatcher, orange crowned warbler, roadrunner, Bewick wren, plain titmouse, shrub jay, California thrasher, green-tailed towhee, rufous-sided towhee, California quail, mountain quail, common poorwill, blue-gray gnatcatcher, Anna's hummingbird, white-crowned sparrow, golden-crowned sparrow, and fox sparrow.

Sagebrush and pinyon pine (4,000 to 8,000 feet—mostly east side): common nighthawk, northern harrier, western kingbird, Say's phoebe, green-tailed towhee, pinyon jay, mountain bluebird, sage sparrow, Brewer's sparrow, sage grouse, and black-billed magpie.

Forest, woodlands and associated meadows (5,000 to 10,000 feet): goshawk, Cooper's hawk, pygmy owl, great gray owl, spotted owl, sharp-shinned hawk, band-tailed pigeon, acorn woodpecker, hairy woodpecker, yellow-bellied sapsucker, white-headed woodpecker, red-breasted nuthatch, Steller's jay, Clark's nutcracker, mountain chickadee, Nashville warbler, solitary vireo, warbling vireo, pileated woodpecker, ruby-crowned kinglet, evening grosbeak, red crossbill, pine siskin, winter wren, junco, brown creeper, yellow-rumped warbler, mountain chickadee, hermit thrush, blue grouse, and western tanager.

Streams and riparian (all elevations): Dip-

ALAN & SANDY CAREY

GEORGE WUERTHNER

Above: American kestrel.
Top right: The golden-mantled ground squirrel looks like a giant chipmunk.
Right: Besides humans, the mountain lion is the mule deer's major predator.

Facing Page: Mule deer.

GEORGE WUERTHNER

CONRAD ROWE

per, harlequin duck, yellowthroat, warbling vireo, yellow warbler, McGillivray's warbler, lazuli bunting, cliff swallow, violet-green swallow, belted kingfisher, black phoebe and wood duck.

Alpine (above 10,000 feet): golden eagle, gray-crowned rosy finch, white-crowned sparrow, white-tailed ptarmigan (introduced and localized in Yosemite), raven, and water pipit.

Mammals

Unlike mountain areas in the Rockies and Canada, the Sierra Nevada has few large mammals. There are no moose. No elk. No caribou. No mountain goat. Most Sierran animals are small, typically rodents. Since most of these species are nocturnal, however, you're not likely to see them. A few are so rare as to be known to science by only a few specimens. For example, the Mount Lyell shrew has only been collected in a few locations in the High Sierra. Nothing is known about its habits or basic ecology.

Two out of four species of mammals extirpated in California—the wolf and the grizzly bear—used to roam in and around the Sierra Nevada. There are numerous historic reports of wolves in the Central Valley. Given the huge herds of elk and antelope reported by early settlers, this does not seem unlikely. As throughout the West, wolves were persecuted and killed at every opportunity by stockmen. Beginning in 1915, the federal government killed wolves as well. The last wolves in California were reported near Tule Lake in the 1920s. Given the abundance of deer in some parts of California, even the Sierra, it is not inconceivable that wolves might be reintroduced into the state again sometime in the future.

The other Sierran animal now extinct in the region, as well as in the state, is the grizzly bear. Grizzlies were undoubtedly more abundant in California than in any other state. Prior to the advent of the European, when acorns, roots, berries, salmon, deer, and elk, were abundant, the grizzly probably had little trouble obtaining enough to eat. Despite this abundance, the grizzly, like the wolf, came into conflict with the stockmen. The grizzly went the same way as the wolf, disappearing before an onslaught of traps, guns and poison. The last California grizzly was seen in Sequoia National Park in 1924. Given that grizzlies can survive in crowded European mountains like the Alps, it is possible that grizzlies could even return to California, if not the Sierra. There is sufficient food to support them, from the oaks

of the foothills to the wildflower gardens of the subalpine, but perhaps not sufficient tolerance yet on the part of humans.

The most common large mammal in the Sierra today is the ubiquitous mule deer. Mule deer are named for their large mule-like ears. In the Sierra, there is an abundance of deer food, from leaves and twigs of shrubs like deerbush, thimbleberry, and manzanita, to the acorns of oaks. Deer on the east side depend on sagebrush, bitterbrush and other shrubs in the winter months. Nevertheless, fire suppression has reduced overall deer food quality.

Most Sierran mule deer are migratory. Some move as much as 50 miles between ranges; some herds cross the entire range twice a year. They winter on the eastern slope of the Sierra and then migrate to the western side for the summer. Mule deer numbers are in decline all across the Sierra, partly as a consequence of the recent prolonged drought of the late 1980s and early 1990s that has reduced forage quality. In many areas, however, particularly on the western slope, subdivisions, malls and roads whittle away at the deer's winter range. The deer herd of the North Kings has declined from 17,000 in the 1950s to 1,900. Similarly, the Bucks Mountain herd in northern California has suffered a 50-percent loss, again attributed to habitat encroachment.

Losses of this magnitude do not bode well for the deer's chief predator—the mountain lion, sometimes called cougar. In a normal year, a mountain lion will kill 50 to 75 deer. While it's true that lions typically take the old, injured or weak, the mountain lion is an excellent predator and will take any animal encountered.

Mountain lions hunt by stealth and ambush, not by racing down prey. As a consequence, mountain lions prefer rugged, broken, rocky terrain where the element of surprise is on their side. Although territorial, with each female having a secure territory, large males have ranges that overlap several females.

Besides deer, the only other large native herbivores in the Sierra are bighorn sheep. Sheep are largely confined to the east-side canyons and alpine ridges, in part because they feed primarily on grasses and shrubs that must be reachable beneath winter snows.

Bighorn sheep were once more abundant perhaps even than deer on the east side of the Sierra. They have been reduced to relict populations in and around Mt. Baxter and Mt.

Williamson, west of Independence. Recent transplants, such as to Lee Vining Canyon, have expanded their distribution somewhat.

Although records are spotty, it appears that sheep occupied the east side of the Sierra more or less continuously from Yosemite south to Walker Pass. There is no doubt that sheep were more widespread—I found a well-decomposed ram's horn on a ridge above Duck Lake south of Mammoth Mountain, where there have been no bighorns for decades.

A number of factors are responsible for the bighorn sheep decline. During the mining days, sheep were hunted to provide fresh meat for isolated mining communities scattered up and down the Sierra. By 1873, bighorns were given protection by the state of California. Far and away the most significant factor in their decline (and still a major obstacle to their full recovery over millions of acres of public lands) is domestic livestock, in particular, domestic sheep.

Domestic sheep affect the wild bighorns in several ways. The domestic animals carry diseases for which bighorns have little immunity. Furthermore, since domestic and wild sheep eat the same plants, heavy overgrazing by domestic animals often reduces the food available for their wild cousins, eventually resulting in the loss of wild sheep. Only in the most rugged sections of the Sierra were sheep able to persist. Today, due to protection and transplants, sheep ranges are expanding. Newly established populations can be found around Wheeler Crest, Mt. Langley and Lee Vining Canyon. Despite these recent expansions, the bighorn sheep population of the entire Sierra is not much more than 300. The Sierran bighorn is classified as a threatened species by the state of California.

The only other large mammal found in the Sierra Nevada is the black bear. Despite its name, many Sierra Nevada black bears are brown in color. Omnivorous, black bears feed on just about anything remotely edible, but settle for grass, roots, berries, and acorns, with insects and meat taken whenever they can get it. In some parts of the Sierra Nevada, the major portion of the bear's diet consists of hot dog buns, watermelon rind, old potato salad, stale cookies and other throwaways from campers.

Bears will go to great lengths to obtain human foods. In this regard, bears display an intelligence unmatched by other animals. They are known to discern the difference between a cooler and a box of books closed in a car, and if

motivated, will tear off the door to obtain said cooler. Even the standard practice of hanging food from a tree when camping in the backcountry does not seem sufficient to dissuade today's sophisticated bear. They know how to untie or bite through ropes, or even shimmy out on branches to grab bags of food.

Although they can be persistent to obtain food, most Sierran black bears are shy and reclusive. There are no "problem" bears, only "problem" people, who through carelessness or ignorance create problems.

Unfortunately for the bear, addiction to human food usually winds up costing the animal its life; human tolerance for bears in and around habitations or camp areas is low. Also, bears accustomed to human food are less wary of humans and more likely to attack or get into trouble—this is one reason National Park Service officials are so strict about food storage regulations. Leaving a cooler out for the night may not seem like a major offense, but it may end up costing a bear its life.

A black bear may double its weight between spring and fall as it puts on fat to carry it through the winter hibernation season. In much of the Sierra, bears do not enter hibernation until December, and they will often emerge again three or four months later. If the winter is unusually mild, some bears will not bother with hibernation at all and may be active all season.

Although we refer to hibernation, these bears are not true hibernators because they do not lower their body temperatures significantly and they can be aroused quite easily. Although bears lose some weight during hibernation, most weight loss occurs after they emerge from their dens and become active in the spring.

Black bears used to range in the forest belt up to 8,000 feet elevation. Bears are now found up to 10,000 feet or more, as they scour the high country for carelessly protected backpackers' food. While the number of bears found in the entire Sierra Nevada is not known, one estimate for Yosemite National Park places bear numbers between 330 and 550 animals.

Several rare animals seldom seen in the Sierra are the wolverine and the fisher. The wolverine, a member of the weasel family, is an extremely rare wanderer of the subalpine forest and alpine zones. This animal looks like a small bear cub, and has a loping gait which enables it to cover miles with little energy. Radio-collared wolverines in Montana were found to travel as much as a hundred miles

MARK LAGERSTROM

BARBARA THOMAS

Above: Snowshoe hares are relatively rare south of Yosemite.
Top right: Steller's jay is common in the west-slope conifer forests.
Bottom right: Pika live year-round in rock piles at higher elevations.

Facing page: Clark's nutcracker is common in the subalpine forests.

GEORGE WUERTHNER

CONRAD ROWE

in a week; thus several sightings or tracks miles apart can be made by the same animal.

The wolverine travels so much, in part, because it subsists upon carrion during much of the winter. When finding food is a matter of odds, odds are increased by traveling a big circuit. Besides the dead meat it can scavenge, the wolverine will attack everything from snowshoe hares to deer. Primarily solitary animals, wolverines are seen together only when adults pair up for mating, or when a female has young.

The fisher is thinner and more cat-like than the wolverine, often slightly darker in coloration, with a deep, rich, chocolate-brown coat. The fisher doesn't eat fish at all; rather it catches squirrels, rabbits and porcupines—a task at which it is particularly adept. More an animal of the forest than of open country like the wolverine, the fisher is a resident of the old-growth and mature forests of the Sierran mid-elevations.

The other member of the weasel family found in the high elevation forests is the long and slender marten. It looks like a small brown cat with an orange throat patch. It is a curious animal, and is as likely to sit and watch you as it is to run away. The bulk of its diet consists of tree squirrels, and voles that reside on the forest floor. The marten also eats berries, and small prey like chipmunks, birds, and other animals when it can capture them.

The marten is seldom seen, but since it is active all winter, one frequently encounters its tracks in the forest, particularly in the red fir forest. Although it roams the landscape year-round, during especially cold periods the marten seeks the insulation found in the pulpy portion of old rotted logs. Since such logs are typically found in old-growth forests, logging of ancient forests may have helped reduce the species over much of the northern Sierra.

Several other members of the weasel family are represented in the Sierra, including the river otter, mink, spotted skunk, striped skunk, short-tailed weasel, and long-tailed weasel. There are some similarities among them. They are long and thin and are primarily predators. Many members of the weasel family have "delayed implantation" of embryos, that is, mating often occurs in the spring or summer, but the embryos delay development until the following spring.

The most aquatic of the weasels is the river otter. It is an excellent swimmer and eats almost anything it catches in rivers, from crayfish to fish. Not surprising, it is associated with rivers and wetlands. Formerly, it was restricted to the foothills, but due to fish stocking of higher-elevation rivers and lakes, it is now found in the mid to high elevations. One of the most playful of animals, it will spend hours sliding down muddy or snowy banks, chasing cohorts about a pool, and swimming just for the sake of swimming. The river otter's voice is a squeaky chip that sounds bird-like. It typically vocalizes only when excited or threatened.

The short- and long-tailed weasels are well distributed throughout the Sierra. The short-tailed weasel tends to favor dense forests and higher elevations, and is rare in the southern Sierra. The long-tailed weasel is more often associated with open areas, from the foothills all the way to the alpine. Both are brown in summer, with cream throats, but their coats change to white in winter. The short-tailed weasel is then called an ermine. Both hunt mice, voles, chipmunks and anything else they can catch, often by following the prey into its burrow. Weasels are curious animals, and will often dart about a log or rock pile to scan people in their territory.

Another very rare mammal is the Sierran red fox, California's only native red fox. There have been only twenty sightings per decade in recent years. (Red fox in the Sacramento Valley were introduced from the eastern United States.) This fox lives primarily in the subalpine region where meadows dot the forest, which provides hunting areas and shelter from storms. In winter, fox travel may be restricted to windblown alpine areas or other open areas.

Once thought to be more abundant, this fox of the high alpine may have suffered declines as a consequence of livestock overgrazing of subalpine and alpine meadows. Loss of cover means fewer hiding places for small mice and voles, the fox's primary food source. Hence, a decline in rodents means fewer foxes. It is also possible that the decline of bighorn sheep, which provided an important source of carrion for the fox, contributed to the fox's decline. One dead sheep is worth a large number of voles in terms of energy.

A fox seen at lower elevations in the chaparral or oak zone is likely to be the gray fox. This fox hunts mice, ground squirrels and rabbits among the ravines and canyons in the foothill country. The gray fox has the unusual habit of climbing trees, and if pursued, will often take to the limbs to escape.

Slightly larger than the gray fox is the coyote, the only other member of the dog family living in the Sierra. The coyote can be found from the foothills to the alpine. It hunts anything it can catch, from mice and voles to a deer fawn. Unlike the foxes, who tend to be silent, coyotes communicate with a variety of yips and howls.

Coyotes are relentlessly killed by stockmen as well as government trappers working for federal Animal Damage Control. This destruction occurs despite research that has demonstrated such control is ineffective; well-fed coyotes simply reproduce at a higher rate. On the other hand, coyotes in unhunted populations establish territories and produce stable social organizations. Fewer young survive to adulthood than in hunted populations. The result is often fewer predation problems.

One of the coyote's prey in the high country is the gray-colored Belding's ground squirrel. Sometimes known as a "picket pin" for its habit of standing erect to search for danger, the squirrel utters loud whistles if danger is perceived. These ground squirrels live in colonies dug in sandy soils at mid to high elevations. They feed on grasses, flowers and shrubs, and hibernate much of the year from October through May.

The California ground squirrel, with burrowing habits similar to the Belding's ground squirrel, is found in drier habitat at lower elevations. It can be distinguished from the Belding's ground squirrel by the light-colored spots on its generally gray back. With its bushy tail, it also might be confused with the western gray squirrel, a tree-dwelling species. The California ground squirrel, however, is more likely to dive into a hole than climb a tree when threatened. Like the Belding's ground squirrel, the California ground squirrel lives in colonies. These squirrels eat a variety of foods, including manzanita seeds, greens, insects, and even meat from road kills. In autumn, they spends most of their time consuming acorns. They may hibernate, depending upon the elevation.

Although coyotes, eagles, and weasels take their toll on Belding's and California ground squirrels, the badger is the most persistent predator. These flattened, squat members of the weasel family are not able to chase down prey, nor clamber about trees in pursuit of a meal, but they will relentlessly dig out each ground squirrel in a colony until few, if any, are left. The badger's flat body enables it to burrow with ease, and its long claws are efficient for excavating. Badgers frequently dig new burrows for themselves, and their abandoned dens are appropriated by everything from foxes and coyotes to rattlesnakes. This

is yet another demonstration of the interconnections among all species. Trapping of badgers, a common practice, may not seem to have an "impact" because badgers are not near extinction, but the ripples of their loss may reverberate through the ecosystem.

Another ground-dweller of the higher elevations is the yellow-bellied marmot, the largest member of the squirrel family. This bushy-tailed animal is common from the alpine zone down to approximately 7,000 feet. The marmot is related to the eastern groundhog, but unlike the groundhog, the marmot is closely associated with rocks instead of dirt burrows. The marmot seldom strays far from the protection of the den, among the rock slides and ledges. Marmots, like the Belding's ground squirrel, live in colonies usually made up of one dominant male, several females, and the young. They eat flowers, grass, and other green foliage. Marmots hibernate during the winter, so must gain all their weight during the short summer growing season or they can die of starvation while hibernating in their burrows.

Seen occasionally scampering among the boulder piles in the alpine and subalpine areas are creatures that look like small rabbits with tiny, round ears. When one emits a squeaky "ekk," you know it's a pika. Pikas eat flowers, grasses and other green vegetation. Since they are active all winter, they also stockpile winter food. Pikas are often called haymakers because they make little piles of grasses and flowers for drying.

The chickaree, or Douglas squirrel, is a louder, noisier rodent of the Sierra. These energetic animals bounce from branch to branch scolding intruders in their territory. Unlike most mammals, these animals are abroad in the daytime, collecting conifer cones and acorns. Like the pika, the chickaree does not hibernate, but lives on food that it stashed during the previous summer and fall. The chickaree generally nests inside a tree cavity, again pointing out the importance of older, "decadent" forests to the survival of many species.

While the chickaree is associated with the dense, higher-elevation forests, the western gray squirrel is found among the blue oaks and black oaks of the foothills and lower-elevation pine forests. Its bushy, plumed tail curls over its back. Although you often see it foraging on the ground, at the first sign of danger it scampers up into the branches of the nearest tree. Given its preference for the oak forests of the Sierra, it's not surprising that this squirrel consumes a great number of

Besides its value as a playground and wildlands sanctuary, the Sierra Nevada produces one of the most valuable resources—water. Without Sierra Nevada water, California would be little more than a desert. It is water from the Sierra that sustains the agricultural base of the Central Valley and helps to quench the thirst of urban dwellers. One source estimates that 48 percent of the run-off in California comes from the Sierra Nevada.

Beginning with the battle to dam the Tuolumne River in Hetch Hetchy Canyon within Yosemite National Park, river after river has seen its flows controlled and diverted to other uses. Tim Palmer, in his book *The Sierra Nevada: A Mountain Journey,* says that the Stanislaus River has 14 major dams, while some 467 dams have been constructed on national forest lands in the Sierra Nevada alone.

WATER AND THE SIERRA

Although flood control, hydroelectric power production and recreation are often the justifications for these dams, the major purpose is water storage to assure adequate supplies for irrigation. Without these impoundments, much of the agricultural development in the Central Valley would be impossible.

These dams and canals have transformed the Central Valley into the most productive agricultural region in the world, but something equally productive was lost as well. At one time, the Sacramento River was California's major salmon producer, with millions of fish running up the river annually. Salmon also ran up the San Joaquin and its tributaries. Today, most salmon runs in these river systems are a thing of the past, and the few salmon left are declining at a rapid rate. Statewide, more than 10 percent of all native fish species are already extinct, and many more are in serious decline.

In addition, prior to the advent of dams and the attendant agricultural development, most Central Valley rivers overflowed their banks, creating vast wetlands that provided food and shelter for millions of birds. Since 1850, California has lost some 4.5 million acres of wetlands, and most of the valley's native grasslands also have been converted to agriculture.

Riparian habitat, the thin green line of vegetation that lines the streams and rivers, has also disappeared. It is estimated that in the 1800s 800,000 acres of riparian forests of giant cottonwood, sycamore, and willow lined the rivers of the Sierra Nevada. Today, fewer than 12,000 acres remain. This loss is due to many factors. Many are related to livestock production—trampling and overgrazing cattle, and dewatering and dam construction to provide water storage for irrigation eventually used to produce forage crops for livestock.

Loss of riparian habitat means the elimination of trees that may be nesting sites for species like the yellow-billed cuckoo and willow fly-catcher—both rare today—and a decrease in the number of large logs that fall into streams. These large fallen trees provide streambank stability, as well as cover for fish and aquatic invertebrates. Furthermore, riparian vegetation acts like a sponge, soaking up water during floods and releasing it during low-water periods of summer. Finally, dams and changes in flow patterns fragment aquatic habitats in much the same fashion that logging can fragment forest ecosystems.

Why do we suffer these losses? Surprising to some who might think of the numerous golf courses and swimming pools in the Los Angeles Basin, it is not for urban uses. In California, urban water supplies account for only 11 percent of the water consumption in the state. Industry uses another six percent, and rural drinking water one percent. The vast majority—some 83 percent of all water used in California—goes for irrigation.

It is not Fresno or Los Angeles that consumes the majority of Sierran run-off. Nor is the water used to grow high-value crops like oranges, grapes or other crops consumed directly by humans. Rather, the lion's share of water taken from Sierran rivers goes to produce food for cows!

According to Marc Reisner, in his book *Overtapped Oasis*, irrigated pasture in California uses 4.2 million acre-feet of water per year, as much as a city of 23 million people. The production of alfalfa, another crop fed to livestock, uses another 4.1 million acre-feet. Thus, the combined irrigation use for livestock feed is equal to the urban water consumption of 48 million people!

Part of the reason low-value crops like alfalfa are grown in the arid Central Valley is that taxpayers often subsidize the production. Taxpayers have paid most, if not all, the costs of dam and canal construction. Plus, by paying higher electrical rates in urban areas, consumers subsidize the electrical pumps used by irrigators, who are frequently charged the lowest rates of all consumers. In most cases, if the government wanted to recover its costs, water would cost from $350 to $900 an acre-foot. Unfortunately, the Bureau of Reclamation sells much of its water for a hundredth of this price, with the average price to agricultural users at $3.50 an acre-foot or less.

Removal of water subsidies and reduction in the use of irrigation water for low-value crops like hay and pasturage would result in almost no reduction in California's total agricultural dollar-value output. There would be water to meet the state's urban needs for decades, without the necessity of additional dams on any Sierra rivers or tributaries. In addition, many rivers that currently run dry due to irrigation dewatering would flow again, increasing the amount available to wildlife, riparian vegetation, and fisheries.

With more water in the Sacramento, San Joaquin, and other rivers, the salmon fisheries might recover, and fish like the Sacramento smelt might not be endangered. While increased flows will not eliminate all the factors that presently threaten California's wildlife and fish, it would go a long way toward ensuring their continued survival.

Such a change in water use may occur. In late 1992, Congress passed a water-use bill sponsored by Representative George Miller of California. The bill requires higher fees for water delivered to agricultural users. Furthermore, the bill specifically requires that minimum flows be maintained to benefit wildlife. In drought years, cuts in water use will be felt more keenly by those in agriculture. Although it is too early to determine how much this reform will benefit wildlife and rivers, it is certainly a step in the right direction.

Above: Cattle near Bridgeport. Hay production and irrigated pasture consume more water in California than any other use.

Facing page: Dam on Gem Lake. Nearly 50 percent of the water in California comes from Sierra Nevada watersheds.

acorns. It will not, however, pass up the opportunity to eat the seeds of conifer cones. It will even eat young birds should it happen upon them.

The golden-mantled ground squirrel, seen in forest meadows, is another member of the squirrel family active in the daytime. It has black and white stripes and looks like a big chipmunk, except its stripes end at the neck, while stripes cover the chipmunk's face as well. Unlike the chickaree, the golden-mantled ground squirrel lives underground in a burrow and hibernates through the winter.

Bats are commonly seen around dusk. There are about 16 species recorded for the Sierra. Many bat species—such as the spotted bat—are rare across their entire range. Others may be abundant. The most common Sierra Nevada bat species are the California bat, long-eared bat, Mexican free-tailed bat, and western pipistrelle.

The bat is primarily insectivorous, and the only mammal that can fly. Bats swoop over water bodies and meadows, nabbing bugs from the air. They can eat their own weight in insects daily. These tiny flying mouse-like animals navigate in the dark by emitting a rapid series of high-frequency squeaks that bounce off nearby obstacles, including insects.

Bats typically have one offspring each. The mothers are protective and affectionate toward their young, licking them clean daily and defending them against danger. The young bat may cling to its mother's fur and go along on daily hunting forays. If disturbed in the brood cave, however, the young bats will sometimes fall or be dropped. The mothers often cannot retrieve them, and as a consequence, the young bats may die. This is one of many reasons why disturbing bat caves is detrimental to the animals.

Like birds, some bats migrate south for the winter, while others seek out caves or other structures for hibernation. During hibernation, fat supplies can become critical. If disturbed during colder months when insects are not available, the bats can die from starvation. Bats have an undeserved nasty reputation, yet they, like all animals, are both interesting and even "cute" once you get to know something about them.

Mammals by Habitat Type

The following list places mammals with their *usual* habitats and elevations. Keep in mind that some species do migrate up and down slope. In addition, within a particular habitat, some species are generalists and widely distributed, while some are strongly associated with a particular habitat type. For example, flying squirrels are almost always associated with old-growth forests, while the coyote, a generalist, ranges from alpine regions to sagebrush desert.

Grasslands, chaparral, and oak savanna (500 to 5,000 feet): gray fox, California ground squirrel, bobcat, ringtail, striped skunk, spotted skunk, raccoon, white-footed mouse, and dusky-footed woodrat.

Sagebrush and pinyon pine (4,000 to 8,000 feet, east side): coyote, badger, pinyon mouse, sagebrush vole, blacktailed jackrabbit, mule deer, mountain lion.

Forest, woodlands and associated meadows (5,000 to 10,000 feet): snowshoe rabbit (hare), western gray squirrel, valley pocket gopher, Allan's pocket gopher, mink, black bear, chickaree (Douglas squirrel), montane vole, lodgepole chipmunk, bushy-tailed woodrat, porcupine, mountain pocket gopher, heather vole, badger, mountain beaver, mule deer, flying squirrel, and mountain lion.

Streams and riparian (all elevations): beaver, mink, river otter, water shrew.

Alpine (above 10,000 feet): pika, white-tailed jackrabbit, yellow-bellied marmot, alpine chipmunk, alpine pocket gopher, and bighorn sheep.

Sleigh below Half Dome in Yosemite National Park in 1925.

FUTURE

Though much of the Sierra Nevada has been given some kind of permanent protection as national park, wilderness, wild and scenic river or other protective designation, the range continues to suffer a slow death that until recently has largely been ignored by all but a few biologists and environmentalists.

The signs of decay are so overwhelming that even the casual observer cannot fail to notice it today. Recently, national and regional publications have focused on the incremental forces slowly dismantling the biological integrity of the entire range.

You need not read these publications to become alarmed. Go see for yourself. A short visit to the Tahoe Basin presents a clear

Right: *Condominiums near June Lake.*

Facing page: *D.L. Bliss State Park at Lake Tahoe. Water pollution threatens the pristine waters. In 1959, you could see a white plate or disk at 100 feet; today the average is 74 feet.*

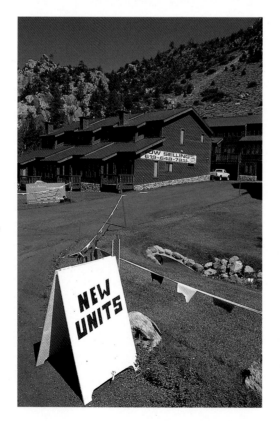

example of the excesses that threaten the Sierra's future. Smog clogs vistas. Forests are dying. Many wildlife species are in decline or gone, even in remote wilderness areas. Some 75 percent of the lake's marshes and wetlands are gone. Subdivisions, malls, and roads sprawl across the landscape. The crystalline waters of Lake Tahoe are losing their clarity. In 1959 you could see a white dinner-plate-sized disk at 100 feet. Today the average is 74 feet.

As bad as the Tahoe Basin may be, it has some advantage over the rest of the Sierra. State and federal agencies are at least attempting to correct and curb some of the worst threats. Such is not the case in much of the rest of the Sierra, although recently there have been several conferences where discussion of coordinated Sierra-wide management has gotten serious review. This offers some encouragement that such a policy may soon be implemented.

Statistics tell the story. Despite claiming a change in policy that promotes "new perspectives," the Forest Service has increased logging on public lands, and timber harvest on private lands has increased as well. For instance, between 1980 and 1989, the cut on Sierra Nevada forestlands jumped from 959 million board feet to 1.6 billion board, a 67 percent increase! As the forest falls before the chain saw, soil erosion is increasing, forest habitat is being fragmented, and scenic vistas are being destroyed. Timber harvest is particularly evident in the northern Sierra, where there is *no* major drainage left that hasn't been sliced by logging roads. Real change in policy may be imminent, however. Early in 1993, the Forest Service announced that it was going to ban clearcuts in the Sierra Nevada national forests for two years in order to protect habitat for the California spotted owl.

Smog is another problem. As valley population has increased, so has the number of cars. Though today's car produces far less pollution, the sheer numbers in California spell trouble. Auto-exhaust pollution from cities like Sacramento and Fresno mixes with smog blown in from the Bay area. All these toxic fumes circulate up and down the Central Valley. Hemmed in by mountains, the polluted brown gunk becomes even more toxic and concentrated. In particular, the area east of Bakersfield has especially dirty air where it piles up against the Sierra. Ozone levels in the mountains may be three to five times greater than levels in Central Valley cities, where the pollution originates.

Such high pollution levels do more than degrade vistas. Studies in Sequoia National Park have found nearly 100 percent occurrence of ozone damage in the Jeffrey pine examined. Growth rates have slowed 11 percent.

Subdivision and growth also impact the Sierra. With 30 million residents in California, people have to live someplace. Increasingly that someplace is in the Sierra Range itself. During the 1980s, six of the state's ten fastest-growing counties were in the Sierra Nevada; Placer County jumped 47 percent and Nevada County 52 percent, for example. Total population in the Sierra region is 800,000—larger than the population of the entire state of Montana. This is a 42 percent increase from just a decade ago. The signs of this growth are everywhere. Developments bring more roads, more power lines, destruction of wildlife habitat and degradation of scenic views.

Although various county, state and federal agencies attempt to deal with each of these problems, no one is taking a coordinated overview of the situation. Part of the problem is jurisdictional battles; there are also funding constraints. On just one transection of the Sierra, from the foothills to the alpine, the land on which you stand could be either privately owned or administered by any of a variety of federal agencies, including the Bureau of Land Management, Forest Service, National Park Service, or the state of California.

Each of these entities has a different interest, agenda, and mandate. Thus, in a national park where natural processes may be paramount, wildfires may be welcome. Immediately adjacent on Forest Service lands, fire suppression is the rule. Yet natural ecological processes like fire do not respect, nor observe, jurisdictional boundaries.

We have learned that habitat fragmentation threatens many species with extinction. Small isolated populations are more likely to go extinct than are larger ones, particularly those that can be periodically reinvigorated by migration from other nearby populations. Yet, some present and past developments and policies are increasing fragmentation of ecosystems. Even our largest national parks are seldom big enough to encompass the full habitat requirements of some of their larger species. Extinctions have already occurred and may continue to occur unless larger blocks of land are managed with biological integrity and function in mind. This doesn't entail prohibiting development and use of every square acre of land. Large parcels of undeveloped land, however, must be connected to other parcels via biologically meaningful corridors.

What is needed is a vision of the Sierra Nevada as the entire geographical entity and ecosystem that it is. Long-term management goals should be designed and coordinated to aid and maximize ecosystem integrity. It is necessary that the entire Sierra Nevada be managed as one ecosystem—the Greater Sierra Nevada Ecosystem. Management coordinated among all agencies should become the norm, with ecosystem preservation and productivity primary considerations.

This approach is already coming into play. For example, wilderness management in the High Sierra is coordinated so that the regulations and goals are the same for each designated wilderness in the area, no matter who administers it. The Tahoe Basin is another example, with a coordinated effort among two states, federal agencies, and local authorities to preserve and enhance the Lake Tahoe area.

Another recent proposal is for a Range of Light National Park, which would take in most of the Sierra Nevada from Yosemite south to the Kern River. A Sierra Nevada Biological Preserve has been discussed. One existing model is Adirondack State Park in New York. Within the park boundaries, state lands and private lands are managed for the common goal of preserving the overall wildness, biological integrity and scenic beauty of the region. People do live in the Adirondacks—there are more than 100 communities—and work and play there as well; however, preserving the area's value as a sustainable biological and social community is paramount. Even a Sierra Nevada Biological Preserve should not exist in isolation. Corridors and links to other ecosystems north, south, and east should be maintained or restored.

These ideas are not beyond physical or scientific possibility. The weak link, if it exists, is politics. Given the urgency of the situation in California, it's possible that even this obstacle may be overcome. If not, the Sierra may soon represent not our grandest conservation achievement and vision, but our greatest failure.

Above: A winter climber at Glacier Divide in Humphrey's Basin in the Inyo National Forest.
Left: A sign of the times—full campground. Yosemite National Park.

Facing page: Meadow flowers and oaks in the San Joaquin River area near Auberry, California.

50 HIGHEST PEAKS

	MOUNTAIN	ELEVATION		MOUNTAIN	ELEVATION
1.	Mt. Whitney	14,495	26.	Mt. Kaweah	13,802
2.	Mt. Williamson	14,375	27.	Mt. Irvine	13,770
3.	North Palisades	14,242	28.	Mt. Winchell	13,768
4.	Starlight	14,200	29.	Black Kaweah	13,765
5.	Polemonium	14,200	30.	Mt. Corcoran	13,760
6.	Mt. Sill	14,163	31.	Mt. Morgan	13,748
7.	Mt. Russell	14,086	32.	Mt. Abbot	13,715
8.	Split Mountain	14,058	33.	Bear Creek Spire	13,713
9.	Middle Palisades	14,040	34.	Mt. Gabb	13,711
10.	Mt. Langley	14,027	35.	Mt. Mendel	13,691
11.	Mt. Tyndall	14,018	36.	Midway Mountain	13,666
12.	Mt. Muir	14,015	37.	Birch Mountain	13,665
13.	Thunderbolt Peak	14,003	38.	Mt. Tom	13,652
14.	Mt. Barnard	13,990	39.	Milestone Mt.	13,641
15.	Mt. Humphreys	13,986	40.	University Peak	13,632
16.	Mt. Keith	13,977	41.	Table Mtn.	13,630
17.	Mt. Stanford	13,963	42.	Mt. Ericsson	13,608
18.	Mt. Le Conte	13,960	43.	Thunder Mountain	13,588
19.	Trojan Peak	13,950	44.	Mt. Brewer	13,570
20.	Disappointment Peak	13,917	45.	Mt. Goddard	13,568
21.	Mt. Agassiz	13,891	46.	Tunnabora Peak	13,565
22.	Junction Peak	13,888	47.	Mt. Dubois	13,559
23.	Mt. Mallory	13,850	48.	Mt. Carillon	13,552
24.	Caltech Peak	13,832	49.	Mt. Bolton Brown	13,538
25.	Mt. Darwin	13,830	50.	Mt. Fiske	13,524

DESIGNATED WILDERNESS AREAS

NAME	ACRES (1992)	PARK/FOREST
Domeland	94,686	Sequoia National Forest
South Sierra	82,30	Sequoia/Inyo national forests
Golden Trout	303,287	Sequoia/Inyo national forests
Sequoia	280,428	Sequoia National Park
Kings Canyon	456,552	Kings Canyon National Park
Jennie Lakes	10,300	Sequoia National Forest
Monarch	44,900	Sierra/Sequoia national forests
Dinkey Lakes	30,000	Sierra National Forest
John Muir	581,000	Inyo/Sierra national forests
Kaiser	22,700	Sierra National Forest
Ansel Adams	230,300	Sierra/Inyo national forests
Yosemite	677,600	Yosemite National Park
Hoover	48,600	Inyo/Toiyabe national forests
Emigrant	112,300	Stanislaus National Forest
Carson-Iceberg	160,000	Stanislaus/Toiyabe national forests
Mokelumne	100,600	Eldorado/Toiyabe/Stanislaus national forests
Desolation	63,475	Eldorado National Forest
Granite Chief	25,700	Tahoe National Forest
Bucks Lake	21,000	Plumas National Forest

Above: A stream near Tioga Road in Yosemite Valley.
Left: View from Glacier Point in Yosemite National Park.

Index

University Peak from Kearsarge Pass in the Inyo National Forest.

George Wuerthner holds degrees in wildlife biology and botany from the University of Montana and a master's degree in science communications from the University of California, Santa Cruz. A former wilderness ranger, teacher, and botanist, he currently earns his living as a freelance writer, photographer, and ecologist. He is the author and photographer of 12 books, among them Montana: Magnificent Wilderness, Nevada Mountain Ranges, Alaska Mountain Ranges, Idaho Mountain Ranges, *and* Yellowstone: A Visitor's Companion. *He frequently contributes to national magazines and journals. His photographs have been exhibited at the Smithsonian Institution and other museums around the country. Wuerthner lives in Livingston, Montana, just north of Yellowstone National Park.*